ESSENTIAL
ANDALUCIA

★ Best places to see 34–55   ■ Featured sight

Córdoba and Jaén Provinces
77–100

Málaga and Cádiz Provinces
131–164

Granada and Almería Provinces
101–130

Seville and Huelva Provinces
165–185

Original text by Des Ha
Updated by Robin Barton

© AA Media Limited 200٤
First published 2008. Repr

ISBN 978-0-7495-6669-2

Published by AA Publishi
office is Fanum House, B
number 06112600.

Colour separation: MRM Graphics Ltd
Printed and bound in Italy by Printer Trento S.r.l.

A04192
Maps in this title produced from mapping © ISTITUTO GEOGRAFICO DE AGOSTINI
S.p.A., NOVARA 2007

About this book

This book is divided into five sections:

The essence of Andalucía pages 6–19
Introduction; Features; Food and drink; Short break

Planning pages 20–33
Before you go; Getting there; Getting around; Being there

Best places to see pages 34–55
The unmissable highlights of any visit to Andalucía

Best things to do pages 56–73
Great places to have lunch; Best markets; Places to take the children; Top activities; Stunning views; Best buys and more

Exploring pages 74–185
The best places to visit in Andalucía, organized by area

Maps All map references are to the maps on the covers. For example, Granada has the reference ✚ 20K – indicating the grid square in which it is to be found

Addresses c/ = Calle (Street)
s/n = sin numero (no number)

Admission prices
Inexpensive (under €5); Moderate (€5–€12); Expensive (over €12)

Hotel prices Prices are per room per night: € budget (under €60); €€ moderate (€60–€150); €€€ expensive (over €150)

Restaurant prices Price for a meal for one person, including wine and service: € budget (under €18); €€ moderate (€18–€35); €€€ expensive (over €35)

Contents

THE ESSENCE OF...

6 – 19

PLANNING

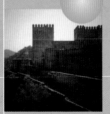

20 – 33

BEST PLACES TO SEE

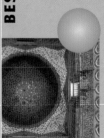

34 – 55

BEST THINGS TO DO

56 – 73

EXPLORING...

74 – 185

The essence of...

Introduction	8–9
Features	10–11
Food and drink	12–15
Short break	16–19

Beyond the beaches of the Costa del Sol, and beyond the world-famous buildings of Seville, Granada and Córdoba, you will find the essence of Andalucía – in the towns and villages of the river plains, amid the peaks and valleys of the Sierras and on the less developed Atlantic and Mediterranean coasts, such as the Costa de la Luz and the eastern section of the Costa de Almería. The vast size of Andalucía, the variety of its landscapes, and the charm and individuality of its people will reward the visitor who is looking for the heart and soul of southern Spain.

features

Andalucía can be all things to all people, provided this intriguing and evocative land is explored with an open mind and with Andalucían enthusiasm.

There is always an alternative here. You can enjoy the crowded high life of the Costa del Sol, find glamour and excitement in Seville and Granada or experience the flavour of North Africa in Almería province. You can stop the world in the shade of a village plaza, become immersed in the colourful festivals of remote villages, wander through cool labyrinths of Moorish streets or stumble across little-known baroque churches and elegant Renaissance buildings in provincial towns. And you can always find solitude among the distant mountains of the Sierra Cazorla or in the green foothills of Las Alpujarras.

GEOGRAPHY

- Andalucía is the most southerly of Spain's 17 political regions.
- The western part of its coastline borders the Atlantic. The eastern coastline borders the Mediterranean.
- About one third of the region is over 600m (1,950ft) high. The highest point is

Mulhacén (3,482m/11,420ft), in the Sierra Nevada.

● Length of coastline: 800km (500 miles).
● Population: 7 million.

AGRICULTURE

● The region produces 2 million tonnes of olives each year, 4 million tonnes of grain and 6.5 million tonnes of grapes.
● Other products include oranges, lemons,

bananas, melons, sugar cane, tomatoes, cucumbers, peppers, potatoes, cotton, tobacco, herbs, spices and flowers.
● *Plasticultura*, the intensive production of fruit and vegetables in huge plastic greenhouses, occupies large areas of the coastal plains east and west of Almería.

INDUSTRY

● Andalucía has mainly light industry, principally located along Guadalquivir Valley.
● There is a concentration of engineering, food processing and textile production in Seville.
● Tourism is a major contributor to the region's economy.

food & drink

Andalucían cuisine reflects the distinctive spirit and ambience of southern Spain through its use of local produce from land and sea, through the needs and tastes of its rural communities and through lingering elements of Moorish cooking. Fish is a popular feature of Andalucían cuisine and fresh vegetables enhance traditional meat dishes, while the cured ham of the Andalucían mountains is renowned. Fresh fruit is also available in abundance. Complementing all of this are the fortified wines: the famous *generosos*, the sherries of southwest Andalucía.

FISH (PESCADOS)

Almería, Málaga, Huelva and numerous coastal villages are noted for their *fritura* (fried fish), but for quality and quantity of fish dishes, Cádiz, Sanlúcar de Barrameda and Jerez de la Frontera are the top spots. Here, fried fish platters of small flat fish and red mullet are

a standard favourite, as is *arroz marinera*, a fish-based *paella*. On the beaches of the Costa del Sol and in Málaga, look out for *chiringuitos*, beach-front bars that specialize in fried or grilled *boquerones* (anchovies), *sardinas* (sardines) and *chanquetes* (whitebait). In more sophisticated restaurants the choice of fish dishes is huge, many based on *atún* (tuna fish), *pez espada* (swordfish) and shellfish such as lobster and prawns.

BEEF AND PORK (CARNE)

The meat stew of Andalucía, the *cocido*, is a popular traditional dish, but one that varies greatly in its ingredients from region to region. Another classic dish is *cola*, or *rabo de toro guisado* (bull's tail stew), a favourite after bullfights but often advertised as oxtail stew. The mountain regions of the Sierra Nevada and Sierra Morena produce the finest cured ham. The *jamón serrano* (mountain ham) of Trevélez in Las Alpujarras, produced from white pigs, is popular, as is the *pata negra* of the Jabugo and Aracena region of the western Sierra Morena, produced from acorn-fed black pigs. Other pork products include *chorizo* (spicy sausage), *salchichón* (salami) and *morcilla* (blood sausage).

WINE (VINO)

Red wine (*tinto*) is the best wine to look for in Andalucía, but is often imported from other parts of Spain, Valdepeñas and Rioja being familiar names to most visitors. There are locally produced red and white wines, and the red wines of Las Alpujarras and other rural areas can be very good. Refreshing drinks are *tinto de verano*, a mix of red wine with ice, and *gaseosa*, a type of lemonade.

Sherry is, of course, the great drink of Andalucía: white wine fortified with alcohol, and subtly refined. Classic sherry comes in the form of *fino* (dry), *amontillado* (medium) and *oloroso* (full-bodied and slightly sweet); *fino* is the ultimate, chilled accompaniment to tapas. Other splendid sherry-like wines are *montilla* from Córdoba province and *manzanillas* from the Sanlúcar de Barrameda area.

Brandy is also produced by the sherry bodegas. Andalucía is Spain's major producer of brandy and is therefore a connoisseur's delight. The great morning pick-me-up is *anís*, a sweet or dry aniseed-based drink.

GAZPACHO

The most famous Andalucían dish is *gazpacho*, a soup that originated as a field-workers' meal and comprised a bread and garlic paste, salted and mixed with olive oil and hot water, and drunk throughout the working day. The soup leftover had vinegar and water added and was drunk cold. *Gazpacho* evolved with the addition of tomatoes, peppers and cucumber, and today there are numerous variations to this excellent starter to a restaurant meal.

DESSERTS (POSTRES)

Meals in Andalucía are often rounded off with fresh fruit, rather than elaborate desserts. *Helado* (ice cream) is also available, and other sweets include cream-filled pastries and crème caramel. For the sweet of tooth, however, the famous Andalucían *dulces*, the mouthwatering sweet cakes that are a lingering legacy of Moorish times, are available in *pastelerías* (cake shops) and are definitely worth trying. You can also buy them in various convents, which produce some exquisite regional specialities.

CHEESE AND EGGS (QUESO AND HUEVOS)

Andalucían cheese is usually produced from goat's milk and sometimes sheep's milk, but rarely from cow's milk. Cheeses can have distinctive local flavours that can be quite strong. Fine cheeses are produced in Aracena and Grazalema, and also in Las Alpujarras and Ronda.

Eggs play an important part in tapas-making and form the basis of the famous *tortilla* (potato-based omelette).

short break

● **Visit the world-famous attractions,** in spite of the crowds: Seville's cathedral and Giralda (➤ 168–169), Granada's Alhambra (➤ 36–37) and Córdoba's Mezquita (➤ 44–45). Be sure to take in the Alcazabas of Almería (➤ 112–113) and Málaga (➤ 134), as well.

● **Check to see whether there is a local festival** in the area you are visiting – and be ready to party.

● **Seek out some of Andalucía's hidden gems.** Visit the Casa de Pilatos in Seville (➤ 168), the Monasterio de la Cartuja in Granada (➤ 107), Sacra Capilla del Salvador in Úbeda (➤ 52–53) and the Iglesia de la Asunción in Priego de Córdoba (➤ 49).

● **Take time to relax** at a café table while watching the world go by.

● **Visit the *pueblos blancos*,** the 'white towns' and hilltop villages of Málaga and Cádiz province, such as Zahara de la Sierra (➤ 54–55), Grazalema (➤ 145), Arcos de la Frontera (➤ 138), Vejer de la Frontera (➤ 149) and Medina Sidonia (➤ 146).

● **Go for a long walk** in Las Alpujarras (➤ 38–39), the Sierra Grazalema (➤ 145), the Sierra Cazorla (➤ 88) or the Sierra Morena (➤ 165).

● **See some flamenco** dancing at a classical performance venue, at a festival or at a *Peñas Flamencas* (a flamenco club). Ask at local tourist offices for details.

● **Eat Andalucían.** Try *gazpacho* (➤ 15), a delicious cold soup that comes in several forms, but is always based on cucumber and tomatoes with olive oil and wine vinegar. Eat fish anywhere, but especially in Cádiz (➤ 139) or Sanlúcar de Barrameda. Above all, indulge yourself in *jamón serrano* or *pata negra*, the delicious cured ham of the Sierras; and sip *fino*, the driest and finest of sherries.

● **Try to visit at least two or three of the following:** Cádiz (➤ 139); Jerez de la Frontera (➤ 42–43); Priego de Córdoba (➤ 48–49); Baeza (➤ 82–83); Úbeda (➤ 52–53).

● **Browse in village shops** that are off the tourist trail. You will often find some fascinating mementoes of your visit that do not carry 'souvenir' prices.

Planning

Before you go   22–25

Getting there   26–27

Getting around   28–29

Being there   30–33

Before you go

WHEN TO GO

JAN	FEB	MAR	APR	MAY	JUN	JUL	AUG	SEP	OCT	NOV	DEC
16°C	17°C	18°C	21°C	23°C	27°C	29°C	29°C	27°C	23°C	19°C	17°C
61°F	63°F	64°F	70°F	73°F	81°F	84°F	84°F	81°F	73°F	66°F	63°F

High season   Low season

Andalucía has a Mediterranean climate: hot, dry summers and mild, wet winters. However, the climate varies by geography as well as the season. Generally, the coast to the west is windier and wetter, with weather fronts sweeping in off the Atlantic, while the east of Andalucía is dry to the extent of desertification around Almería. Low-lying inland areas, such as Seville and Córdoba, get extremely hot in July and August but mountain regions can remain cool until well into the summer; in the winter the mountains are usually cold and wet and often snowbound.

Consider when local festivals are taking place – it is very hard to find accommodation during festivals such as *Semana Santa* (Holy Week) in Seville. In the winter many coastal resorts close down for a month or two.

WHAT YOU NEED

		Some countries require a passport to remain valid for a minimum period (usually at least six months) beyond the date of entry – contact their consulate or embassy or your travel agency for details.	UK	Germany	USA	Netherlands
●	Required					
○	Suggested					
▲	Not required					
Passport (or National Identity Card where applicable)			●	●	●	●
Visa (regulations can change – check before your journey)			▲	▲	▲	▲
Onward or Return Ticket			▲	▲	●	▲
Health Inoculations			▲	▲	▲	▲
Health Documentation (➤ 23, Health Insurance)			●	●	●	●
Travel Insurance			○	○	○	○
Driving Licence (national – EU format/Spanish translation/international)			●	●	●	●
Car Insurance Certificate (if own car)			●	●	●	●
Car Registration Document (if own car)			●	●	●	●

WEBSITES

www.spain.info
Spain's national tourist office

www.andalucia.org
Regional tourism website

TOURIST OFFICES AT HOME

In the UK
Spanish Tourist Office,
22/23 Manchester Square,
London W1M 5AP
☎ 020 7486 8077

In the USA
Tourist Office of Spain,

35th Floor, 666 Fifth Avenue,
New York, NY 10103
☎ 212 265 8822
and
Tourist Office of Spain,
8383 Wilshire Boulevard,
Suite 960, Beverley Hills, CA 90211
☎ 323 658 7188

HEALTH INSURANCE

EU nationals can get reduced-cost emergency medical treatment with the European Health Insurance Card (EHIC), although medical insurance is still advised and is essential for all other visitors. Visitors from the US should check their insurance coverage.

ADVANCE PASSENGER INFORMATION

Security rules introduced in June 2007 mean that all passengers on all flights to and from Spain must now supply Advance Passenger Information (API) to the Spanish authorities: full given names, surname, nationality, date of birth and travel document details (passport number). Airlines will be responsible for collecting the compulsory information either through their websites, travel agents, or airport check-in desks.

TIME DIFFERENCES

GMT 12 noon	Spain 1PM	Germany 1PM	USA (NY) 7AM	Netherlands 1PM	Italy 1PM

Spain is one hour ahead of Greenwich Mean Time (GMT+1) in winter, but summer time (GMT+2) operates from late March until late October.

NATIONAL HOLIDAYS

1 Jan *New Year's Day*

6 Jan *Epiphany*

28 Feb *Andalucían Day (regional)*

Mar/Apr *Maundy Thursday, Good Friday, Easter Monday*

1 May *Labour Day*

24 Jun *San Juan (regional)*

25 Jul *Santiago (regional)*

15 Aug *Assumption of the Virgin*

12 Oct *National Day*

1 Nov *All Saints' Day*

6 Dec *Constitution Day*

8 Dec *Feast of the Immaculate Conception*

25 Dec *Christmas Day*

WHAT'S ON WHEN

January 6 Jan: *Cabalgata de los Reyes Magos*, Málaga. An Epiphany parade.

February Pre-Lenten, week-long *Carnaval* in many Andalucían towns and cities, including Antequera, Cádiz, Carmona, Córdoba, Málaga.

March/April *Semana Santa* (Holy Week). Follows Palm Sunday and is one of the most powerful and passionate celebrations in the world. It is most colourful and dramatic in Seville.

April This is the month of the most exuberant *ferias* – Seville's is among the best and biggest in Spain. It is held one or two weeks after Easter, but always in April. Vejer de la Frontera holds an Easter Sunday *feria*, with bull-running through the streets.

May First week: Horse Fair, Jerez de la Frontera.

Fiesta de los Patios. Córdoba's fabulous private patios are open to the public in early May.

First weekend of May: *Las Cruces de Mayo*. Córdoba's most popular festival, with street dancing and fully booked hotels.

Romería del Rocío (Whitsun). Vast numbers congregate at the village of El Rocío, Huelva, to celebrate the *La Blanca Paloma*, the 'White Dove', the Virgen del Rocío.

Thursday after Trinity Sunday: *Corpus Christi*. Festivals and bullfights in Seville, Granada, Ronda, Zahara de la Sierra, and at smaller towns.

June Second week: *Feria de San Barnabé*, Marbella.

13–14 Jun: *San Antonio Fiesta*, Trevélez, Las Alpujarras. Mock battles between Moors and Christians.

July *La Virgen del Carmen*, Fuengirola, Estepona, Marbella, Nerja and Torremolinos. Celebrates the patron saint of fishermen.

August 5 Aug: *Mulhacén Romería*, Trevélez. Midnight procession to Sierra Nevada's highest peak.

13–21 Aug: *Feria de Málaga*. Very lively fiesta.

Mid-Aug: Horse races along the sandy beaches at Sanlúcar de Barrameda.

Third weekend: *Fiesta de San Mames*, Aroche. Friendly village fiesta.

September 7 Sep: *Romería del Cristo de la Yedra*, Baeza. Street processions and entertainment.

6–13 Sep: *Festival Virgen de la Luz*, Tarifa.

First two weeks: *Pedro Romero Fiestas*, Ronda. Celebration of the famous bullfighter.

October 15–23 Oct: *Feria de San Lucas*, Jaén. The city's main festival.

6–12 Oct: *Feria del Rosario*, Fuengirola. Horse riding and flamenco.

December 28 Dec: *Fiesta de los Verdiales*, Málaga province. Lively, theatrical and musical event in villages to the north of Málaga.

Pride and Passion

The *festival* (festival), the *feria* (fair) and the *fiesta* (holiday) are at the heart of Andalucían culture. The *festival* is often religious in its elements. The *feria* originates from livestock fairs and today is significant for much flamboyant horsemanship. *Romerías* are religious processions culminating in a picnic. The line between the religious and the secular is blurred in Andalucía, and the same earthy passion is expressed during the most intense religious periods, such as Holy Week, as at the life-affirming spring celebrations. Celebration is so inherent to life in Andalucía that visitors are likely to find themselves with some form of local *feria* or *festival* due in their locality. Do not miss out on them if you want to get near to the absolute, exuberant, passionate essence of Andalucía.

Getting there

BY AIR

Almería Airport

10km (6 miles) to city centre

25 minutes

20 minutes

20 minutes

Málaga Airport

10km (6 miles) to city centre

12 minutes

20 minutes

20 minutes

Seville Airport

8km (5 miles) to city centre

N/A

20 minutes

20 minutes

Andalucía's principal airports are Málaga and Seville, with low-cost airlines also flying to Almería and Granada. Málaga's airport is the region's largest and will double in size by 2010, with the addition of new terminal buildings and a new runway. The work taking place at Málaga will cause delays to those driving to the airport, so factor in extra time to negotiate the traffic. New security measures introduced to Spanish airports in 2006 and 2007 may slow down check-in times; confirm the current regulations with your airline before setting off for the airport.

Most of Spain's airports are managed by Aena (☎ 902 404 704; www.aena.es); in Andalucía these airports are Almería, Córdoba, Granada, Jerez, Málaga and Seville. Updates, flight information and airport maps can be downloaded from the organization's website.

Flights to Andalucía from various British airports, including London's Heathrow, Gatwick, Luton and Stansted airports, and Bristol, Bournemouth, Southampton, Manchester, Glasgow and Birmingham, take less than three hours. Many other European countries have direct flights to Andalucían airports, but flights from North America will be routed via

Madrid. Fares for budget airline flights from Europe will typically be less expensive than the corresponding rail fare or the cost of driving; there may also be favourable car rental rates from the airline. Package holidays booked through an agent are another option, although these are diminishing in popularity due to number of self-booked holidays that can be found on the internet.

BY CAR

Outside of the cities and the fast, narrow A7 coast road, driving in Andalucía can be enjoyable. Fast, well-maintained motorways (A-roads) connect Andalucía with Madrid, Valencia and other major cities.

BY TRAIN

Reaching Andalucía by train typically involves taking a train from Madrid to Seville or Córdoba. Spain's extensive train network, operated by RENFE (www.renfe.es), is one of the least expensive in Europe. Tickets can be purchased in advance from travel agents, from RENFE's website or at rail stations. A train journey from the UK to Andalucía will take more than 24 hours and will involve several changes – at least at Paris and Madrid.

BY FERRY

There are ferry services to Bilbao and Santander, on Spain's northwest coast, from the British ports of Plymouth and Portsmouth. A crossing typically takes between 24 and 34 hours in a car ferry operated by P&O Ferries (www.poferries.com) or Brittany Ferries (www.brittany-ferries.co.uk). You then need to drive through western and central Spain to reach Andalucía. There are also ferry services from Tangier, Ceuta and Melilla in Morocco to Tarifa, Algeciras, Málaga, Motril, Almería and Gibraltar.

Getting around

PUBLIC TRANSPORT

Internal Flights The national airline, Iberia (www.iberia.com), plus the smaller Aviaco, operate an extensive network of internal flights. For reservations on domestic flights ☎ 902 40 05 00.

Trains Services are provided by the state-run company – RENFE (www.renfe.es). Fares are usually relatively inexpensive. For rail inquiries for Almería ☎ 950 23 18 22; for Cádiz, Córdoba, Granada, Seville and Málaga ☎ 902 24 02 02 (this line has an English-language option).

Buses Andalucía has a comprehensive and reliable bus network operated by different companies along the coast and to inland towns and villages. Fares are very reasonable. Go to the local bus station for details of routes: Almería ☎ 950 26 20 98; Cádiz ☎ 950 21 00 29; Córdoba ☎ 957 40 40 40; Granada ☎ 958 18 54 80; Seville ☎ 954 41 71 11; Málaga ☎ 952 35 00 61.

Urban Transport Traffic in the cities of Andalucía generally, and in the main towns and resorts of the Costa del Sol in particular, is normally heavy, especially in summer, but public transport in the form of buses is generally good.

TAXIS

Only use taxis that display a licence issued by the local authority. Taxis show a green light when available for hire. They can be flagged down in the street. In cities and large towns taxis are metered; where they are not, agree the price of the journey in advance.

FARES AND TICKETS

Train services are categorised according to the speed of the service: the high-speed AVE trains serve just Cordoba and Seville in Andalucía while slower, regional services connect smaller towns and cities. Train tickets can be purchased in advance online at www.renfe.es, or from travel agents. Collect your pre-purchased ticket from a station; bring ID and the credit card you used to make the booking. It is worth booking in advance for long-distance trips at peak times on popular tourist routes. Tickets can also be purchased from counters and machines in stations.

Bus services are managed by numerous local companies; timetables are available from local tourist offices and tickets can be purchased at the point of travel. Buses are a good way of travelling from village to village but trains are preferable for journeys of an hour or longer.

DRIVING
- Speed limits on *autopistas* (toll motorways) and *autovías* (free motorways): 120kph (74mph); dual carriageways and roads with overtaking lanes: 100kph (62mph).
- Speed limits on country roads: 90kph (56mph).
- Speed limits on urban roads: 50kph (31mph); in residential areas: 20kph (12mph).
- Take care on the N340 coastal highway – a particularly dangerous road.
- Seatbelts must be worn in front seats at all times and in rear seats where fitted.
- Random breath-testing. Never drive under the influence of alcohol.
- Fuel (*gasolina*) is available as either *sin plomo* (unleaded, 95 and 98 octane) or *gasoleo/gasoil* (diesel). Petrol prices are fixed by the government and are lower than those in the UK. Most garages take credit cards.
- If you break down in your own car and are a member of an AIT-affiliated motoring club, call the Real Automóvil Club de España, or RACE (☎ 915 94 74 00; www.race.es) for assistance. If the car is hired you should follow the instructions in the documentation; most international rental firms provide a rescue service.

CAR RENTAL
The leading international car rental companies operate in the main cities and on the Costa del Sol. You can hire a car in advance (essential at peak periods) either direct or through a travel agent.

Being there

TOURIST OFFICES

Almería
Parque Nicolás Salmerón s/n
☎ 950 27 43 55

Baeza
Plaza del Pópulo s/n
☎ 953 74 04 44

Cádiz
Avenida Ramón de Carranza s/n
☎ 956 25 86 46

Córdoba
c/ Torrijos 10 ☎ 957 47 12 35

Granada
Corral del Carbón,
c/ Libreras 2 ☎ 958 22 59 90
Municipal Tourist Office:
Plaza Mariana Pineda 10
☎ 958 24 71 28

Huelva
Avenida de Alemania 12
☎ 959 25 74 03

Jaén
Maestra 13 ☎ 953 24 26 24

Málaga
Pasaje de Chinitas 4
☎ 952 21 34 45

Ronda
Plaza de España 1 ☎ 952 87 12 72

Seville
Avda de Kansas City s/n, Estación
de Santa Justa ☎ 954 53 76 26

Úbeda
Bajo de Marqués 4 ☎ 954 75 08 97

MONEY

Spain's currency is the euro, which is divided into 100 cents. Coins come in denominations of 1, 2, 5, 10, 20 and 50 cents, 1 and 2 euros, and notes come in 5, 10, 20, 50, 100, 200 and 500 euro denominations.

TIPS/GRATUITIES

Yes ✓ No ✗	
Restaurants (if service not included)	✓ 5–10%
Cafés/Bars (if service not included)	✓ change
Taxis	✓ 2–3%
Chambermaids/Porters	✓ change
Toilets	✓ change

POSTAL SERVICES

Post offices (*correos*) are generally open Mon–Fri 9–2, Sat 9–1; in main centres they may open for longer. Málaga's main post office is at Avenida de Andalucía 1 (☎ 902 197 197; www.correos.es). Stamps (*sellos*) can also be bought at tobacconists (*estancos*).

TELEPHONES

All telephone numbers throughout Spain now consist of nine digits and you must always dial all nine digits. Local calls are inexpensive. Although you can pay with coins, it is quicker and easier to buy a phonecard from any *estanco* (tobacconist). Many phones also take credit cards. Long-distance calls are cheaper from a booth than from your hotel. Directory information is 003.

International Dialling Codes

From Spain to:
UK: 00 44
Germany: 00 49

USA: 00 1
Netherlands: 00 31
Ireland: 00 353

INTERNET SERVICES

Many mid- and high-priced hotels offer some sort of internet access. Most towns and cities have at least one internet café, but wireless broadband (wi-fi) is less common than in some countries. Expect to pay for internet access in hotels and cafés, but rates should be reasonable.

EMBASSIES AND CONSULATES

UK ☎ 952 352 300 (Málaga)
Germany ☎ 952 21 24 42 (Málaga)
Ireland ☎ 954 21 63 61 (Seville)

Netherlands ☎ 952 27 99 54 (Málaga)
USA ☎ 952 47 48 91 (Fuengirola)

HEALTH ADVICE

Sun Advice Try to avoid the midday sun and always use a high-factor sun cream. The sunniest months are July and August, when daytime temperatures often reach more than 30°C (86°F).

Medicines Prescriptions, non-prescription drugs and medicines are available from pharmacies (*farmácias*), distinguished by a large green cross. They are able to dispense many drugs that would be available only on prescription in other countries.

Safe Water Tap water is chlorinated and generally safe to drink; however, unfamiliar water may cause mild abdominal upsets. Mineral water (*agua mineral*) is inexpensive and widely available. It is sold *sin gas* (still) and *con gas* (carbonated).

PERSONAL SAFETY

Snatching of handbags and cameras, pick-pocketing, theft of unattended baggage and car break-ins are the principal crimes against visitors. Any crime or loss should be reported to the national police force (Policía Nacional), who wear blue uniforms.

Some precautions:

- Do not leave valuables on the beach or poolside.
- Place valuables in a hotel safety-deposit box.
- Wear handbags and cameras across your chest.
- Avoid lonely, seedy and dark areas at night.

ELECTRICITY

The power supply is 220/230 volts (in some bathrooms and older buildings it is 110/120 volts). Buildings have round two-hole sockets taking round plugs of two round pins. British visitors will need an adaptor and US visitors a voltage transformer.

OPENING HOURS

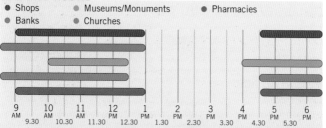

● Shops ● Museums/Monuments ● Pharmacies
● Banks ● Churches

9 AM · 9.30 · 10 AM · 10.30 · 11 AM · 11.30 · 12 PM · 12.30 · 1 PM · 1.30 · 2 PM · 2.30 · 3 PM · 3.30 · 4 PM · 4.30 · 5 PM · 5.30 · 6 PM

LANGUAGE

Spanish is one of the easiest languages. All vowels are pure and short. Some useful tips on speaking: 'c' is lisped before 'e' and 'i', otherwise hard; 'h' is silent; 'j' is pronounced like a gutteral 'j'; 'r' is rolled; 'v' sounds more like 'b'; and 'z' is the same as a soft 'c'. English is widely spoken in the principal resorts but you will get a better reception if you at least try communicating with Spaniards in their own tongue.

hotel	*hotel*	reservation	*reserva*
room	*habitación*	rate	*precio*
single/double	*individual/doble*	breakfast	*desayuno*
one/two nights	*una/dos noche(s)*	toilet	*lavabo*
per person	*por persona*	bath	*baño*
per room	*por habitación*	shower	*ducha*
bank	*banco*	coin	*moneda*
exchange office	*oficina de cambio*	foreign currency	*moneda extranjera*
post office	*correos*	change money	*cambiar dinero*
cashier	*cajero*	pound sterling	*libra esterlina*
money	*dinero*	American dollar	*dólar americano*
restaurant	*restaurante*	tourist menu	*menú turístico*
bar	*bar*	wine list	*carta de vinos*
table	*mesa*	lunch	*almuerzo*
menu	*carta*	dinner	*cena*
aeroplane	*avión*	bus stop	*parada de autobús*
airport	*aeropuerto*	ticket	*billete*
flight	*vuelo*	single/return	*ida/ida y vuelta*
train	*tren*	timetable	*horario*
train station	*estación ferrocarril*	non-smoking	*no fumadores*
yes	*sí*	goodbye	*adiós*
no	*no*	good night	*buenas noches*
please	*por favor*	excuse me	*perdóneme*
thank you	*gracias*	help!	*ayuda!*
hello	*hola*	today	*hoy*

Best places to see

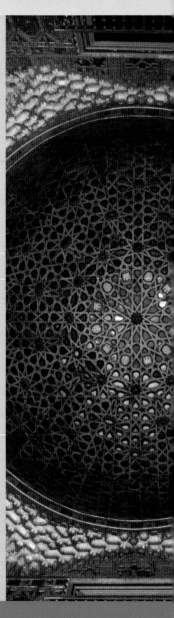

La Alhambra, Granada   36–37

Las Alpujarras   38–39

Gruta de las Maravillas, Aracena   40–41

Jerez de la Frontera   42–43

La Mezquita, Córdoba   44–45

Parque Natural el Torcal   46–47

Priego de Córdoba   48–49

Reales Alcázares, Seville   50–51

Úbeda   52–53

Zahara de la Sierra   54–55

1 La Alhambra, Granada

www.alhambra-patronato.es

La Alhambra is the greatest expression of Moorish culture in Spain, and is one of the world's most spectacular heritage sites.

The Alhambra stands on top of Granada's Sabika Hill, against the background of the often snow-covered massif of the Sierra Nevada. The walled complex is nearly 700m (760 yards) long and about 200m (220 yards) wide. Its name is a corruption of the Arabic *Al Qal'a al-Hamrá*, 'the red castle', a reference to the ruby-red sandstone walls of the Alcazaba, the original fortress built by the 11th-century Emirs of Córdoba. The Alhambra's other Islamic buildings were constructed during the 13th and 14th centuries by the Nasrites, the last great Moorish rulers, at a time when most of Andalucía, except Granada, had fallen to the 'Reconquest' of Catholic Spain.

There are four groups of buildings: the Alcazaba, on the western escarpment of Sabika; the Casa Real, the 14th-century Royal Palace of the Sultans; the Palace of Carlos V, a 15th-century Renaissance addition; and the Palacio del Generalife, the gardens and summer palace of the Sultans.

The heart of the Alhambra is the Casa Real, which reflects the ingenious manipulation of space and light and of cool water that was the special gift of Moorish architecture. The walls and roofs of its enthralling salons have exquisite stucco work, tiling and decorations that will take your breath away.

➕ *Granada 4b* ✉ c/ Real s/n ☎ 902 44 12 21 🕐 Mar–Oct daily 8:30–8; floodlit visits Tue–Sat 10pm–11:30pm. Nov–Feb daily 8:30–6; floodlit visits Fri, Sat 8pm–9:30pm 💷 Expensive; free Sun after 3pm. Free daily to visitors with disabilities and senior citizens 🍴 Drinks and snack kiosk 🚌 Alhambrabus every 10 minutes: Plaza Isabel la Católica–Plaza Nueva ❓ Pre-book your Alhambra entry, as numbers are restricted. Tickets can be reserved by phoning 902 22 44 60 (in Spain) or +34 915 37 91 78 (from abroad). You can also book in any BBVA bank branch

2 Las Alpujarras

The southern foothills of the Sierra Nevada, known as Las Alpujarras, were the last stronghold of Moorish influence in medieval Spain.

The hills of Las Alpujarras descend in green waves to the arid river valleys of the Río Guadalfeo in the west and the Río Andarax in the east. On the south side of these valleys lie the Sierra de Contraviesa

and the Sierra de Gádor, mountain barriers that shut out the developed Almerían coast. A more ancient people than the Moors first carved out cultivation terraces and irrigation channels on the hillsides, but the region's history as the final enclave of the *Moriscos*, nominally Christianized Moors, has given Las Alpujarras much of its romantic appeal.

This is complex and enchanting countryside, which offers superb walking. Driving in Las Alpujarras can also be a pleasure (➤ 116–117), provided you accept that it may take you all day to drive 50km (31 miles) along the great shelf of hills. Narrow, serpentine roads bend to the terraced slopes and sink discreetly into the valleys. Ancient villages and hamlets such as Bayárcal, Yegen and Bérchules invite relaxing halts. The flat-roofed, North African-style houses of the villages are painted white now, but originally the bare stone walls merged with the landscape.

At the heads of the deepest western valleys in the 'High Alpujarras' lie popular villages such as Trevélez, 'capital' of *jamón serrano*, the famous cured ham of the mountains. Further west is the Poqueira Gorge, a deep valley striking into the heart of the Sierra Nevada. Clinging to its slopes are the charming villages of Pampaneira, Bubión and Capileira, from where the wild country of the Sierra is easily reached on foot.

✚ 21K ✉ Southern Sierra Nevada, Granada province
🍴 Bars and restaurants in most villages (€–€€)
🚌 Regular service Granada–Alpujarra ☎ 958 18 54 80
❓ *Fiesta de San Antonio,* Trevélez, 13–14 Jun; Pilgrimage to the peak of Mulhacén from Trevélez, 5 Aug

3 Gruta de las Maravillas, Aracena

The spectacular limestone formations of Aracena's underground cave system, the Gruta de las Maravillas, are the finest in Andalucía.

Aracena's limestone caves, the Gruta de las Maravillas (Grotto of Marvels, or Cavern of the Wonders) comprise nearly 1.2km (0.75 miles) of illuminated galleries and tunnels that are open to the public. These galleries link 12 spectacular caverns, where limestone deposits have formed stalactites and stalagmites and densely layered flows of calcium carbonate known as tufa. There are six small lakes within the system and the whole is linked by paved walkways, ramps and steps. Carefully arranged lighting adds to the effect and piped music, specially written for the site, murmurs in the background. (Note that the caves can be quite chilly, so take a sweater or jacket.)

Guided tours of the caves are accompanied by commentary in Spanish, but non-Spanish speakers will still enjoy a visually stunning experience. Stay near the back of the crowd and you will have time to admire the fantastic natural architecture that often seems to mirror, with grotesque exaggeration, the intricate decoration of baroque altars and Mudéjar façades of Andalucían churches. The caverns all have special names, and the guide points out lifelike figures and faces on the convoluted walls and roofs. The final cavern, known famously as the *Sala de los Culos*, the 'Room of the

Backsides', is exactly that: a hilarious extravaganza of comic rude bits, of huge limestone phalluses and entire tapestries of pink tufa buttocks. You will hear groups of elderly Spanish ladies at the head of the throng shriek with laughter as they reach this part of the tour.

🞥 4C ✉ Pozo de la Nieve s/n ☎ 959 12 82 06 🕓 Daily 10:30–1:30, 3–6. Mon–Fri tours every hour, Sat–Sun tours every half-hour 👋 Moderate 🍴 Casas (▶ 180)
🚌 Regular services Huelva–Aracena, Seville–Aracena
❓ Book tickets at the tourist centre opposite caves entrance. At busy periods your entry time may be an hour or two after booking

4 Jerez de la Frontera

www.turismojerez.com

Jerez de la Frontera has given its name to sherry, one of the most popular drinks in the world. It is also a centre of equestrianism and flamenco.

The rich chalky soil of the Jerez area supported vine-growing from the earliest times. Today the coastal region that lies south of a line between Jerez and Sanlúcar de Barrameda is the official sherry-producing area, the Marco de Jerez. The famous sherry-producing bodegas of Jerez are where fermented wine, produced mainly from white Palomino grapes, is stored and transformed into sherry, and where brandy is also produced. Tours of bodegas end with a pleasant tasting session, confirming the precise distinctions between dry *fino* and the darker and sweeter *oloroso* and *amontillado*.

Jerez's other famous institution is the Real Escuela Andaluza del Arte Ecuestre (Royal Andalucían School of Equestrian Art) at Avenida Duque de Abrantes: the horse-riding displays should not be missed. Jerez has excellent cafés, restaurants and shopping, especially in its pedestrianized main street, Calle Larga. Rewarding visits can be made to the restored 11th-century Alcázar and Arab Baths, the delightful Plaza de la Asunción and the Barrio Santiago, Jerez's old gypsy, or *gitano,* quarter, with its narrow lanes and old churches. In the Barrio you can visit the Museo Arqueológico (Archaeological Museum) in Plaza del Mercado, or see archive material and audio-visual presentations about flamenco at the Centro Andaluz de Flamenco in the Plaza de San Juan.

✚ 13J ✉ 35km (22 miles) northeast of Cádiz, 83km (52 miles) south of Seville 🚊 Plaza de la Estación s/n ☎ 956 34 23 19 🚌 Plaza de la Estación ☎ 956 34 52 07 ❓ *Semana Santa* (Holy Week), Mar/Apr; Horse Fair, early May; *Vendemia*, wine festival, early Sep
ℹ c/ Larga s/n ☎ 956 32 47 47; 956 33 96 28

43

5 La Mezquita, Córdoba

Of all the Moorish buildings to survive in Andalucía, the Great Mosque of Córdoba is the most haunting and the most Islamic in its forms.

The Mezquita (Mosque) of Córdoba was begun in 785 and expanded and embellished during the following two centuries. You enter the complex by the Patio de los Naranjos, the Courtyard of the Orange Trees, where numerous fountains once

sparkled in the dappled shade and where Muslim worshippers carried out ritual ablutions. The mosque itself is then entered through the modest Puerta de las Palmas. Immediately, you are amid the thickets of columns and arches that are the enduring symbol of the Mezquita. Smooth pillars of marble, jasper and onyx, plundered from the building's Roman and Visigothic predecessors, supplement the total of more than 1,200 columns supporting the horseshoe arches of red brick and white stone. At the far end of the vast interior you will find the *mihrab*, the prayer niche of the mosque, a breathtaking expression of Islamic art.

At the very centre of the Mezquita stands the 1523 Renaissance cathedral of Carlos V, an intrusion that reflected Christian pride rather than piety. Carlos later admitted that the addition of the cathedral had 'destroyed something that was unique in the world'. The cathedral's presence is cloaked by the surrounding pillars of the mosque and made somehow less obvious, although it is the focus of worship today. Its carved mahogany choir stalls are outstanding and there are other striking baroque features, but it is the Islamic Mezquita, with its forest of columns and swirling arches, that is most compelling.

🔁 8D ✉ c/ Torrijos 10 ☎ 957 47 05 12 🕐 Apr–Sep Mon–Sat 10–7, Sun 2–7; Oct–Mar Mon–Sat 10–5, Sun 2–7 💶 Moderate 🍴 Restaurante Bandolero, c/ Torrijos 6 (€€) 🚌 Avenida de América

6 Parque Natural el Torcal

El Torcal, with its spectacular rock formations, is one of the most remarkable of Andalucía's Natural Parks.

The limestone pinnacles and cliffs of the Sierra del Torcal cover an area of 1,171ha (2,890 acres). The name *Torcal* derives from the word for 'twist' and aptly sums up the maze of narrow vegetation-filled gullies and ravines among the towering reefs and pillars of rock. From the visitors' car park there are several waymarked circular walking routes through the labyrinth. The shortest route tends to be crowded but there are longer circular routes, and well-worn paths into the labyrinth can be followed, and then retraced. An early morning or late afternoon visit is recommended.

The dense undergrowth is formed from holm oak, hawthorn, maple and elder; ivy clings to the rock faces. Countless flowering plants include saxifrage, peony, rock buttercup, rock rose, thistle and orchid. El Torcal's isolation supports a rich bird life that includes the great grey shrike, vultures and eagles, as well as many small perching birds. There is a good chance of spotting the harmless but fierce-looking ocellated lizard, the largest lizard in Europe.

A short path near the reception centre at the entrance to El Torcal leads to the Mirador de las Ventanillas, a spectacular viewpoint.

✚ 18K ✉ 13km (8 miles) south of Antequera ☎ Reception centre: 952 03 13 89 🕐 Daily 10–5 🍴 Café (€€)

7 Priego de Córdoba

www.turismodepriego.com

The charming town of Priego de Córdoba is rich in baroque architecture and offers a rare insight into provincial Andalucía.

From Priego's central square, the handsome Plaza de la Constitución, the broad Calle del Río leads southeast past the churches of Our Lady of Anguish and Our Lady of Carmen to a peaceful square with two splendid fountains. These are the

16th-century Fuente del Rey, with its sculpture of Neptune and Amphitrite, and the more restrained Renaissance fountain, the Fuente de la Virgen de la Salud.

From busy Plaza Andalucía, adjoining the Plaza de la Constitución, walk northeast down Solana and through the Plaza San Pedro to a junction with Calle Doctor Pedrajas. To the left is a 16th-century slaughterhouse, the Carnicerías Reales, beautifully preserved with an arcaded patio. Turning right along Calle Doctor Pedrajas brings you to the Plaza Abad Palomina and the privately owned Moorish Castillo. Priego's greatest baroque monument, the Iglesia de la Asunción (Church of the Ascension), is at the far corner of the square. Its plain, whitewashed exterior gives no indication of the treasures inside: a beautifully carved *retablo* (altarpiece) and a spectacular *sagrario* (sacristy), an extravaganza of white stucco, frothing with emblems and statues beneath a cupola pierced by windows.

From delightful little Plaza de Santa Ana, alongside the church, head into the Barrio de la Villa down Calle Real, and wander through this old Moorish quarter. Stroll along Calle Jazmines to find the Paseo de Adarve, an airy Moorish promenade with superb views to the surrounding hills.

✚ 19J ✉ 65km (40 miles) southeast of Córdoba
🚌 Regular service Granada–Priego, Córdoba–Priego. Estación de Autobuses, c/ San Marcos 🛈 Carrera de las Monjas 1
☎ 957 70 06 25 🕔 Mon–Sat 10–2, 4–7, Sun 10–2

8 Reales Alcázares, Seville

www.patronato-alcazarsevilla.es

The Royal Palaces are a fine example of Mudéjar building – Moorish-influenced post-Conquest architecture.

After Seville fell to Christian forces in 1248, Spanish king Pedro the Cruel reshaped and rebuilt much of the city's original Alcázar in Mudéjar style. It is this version that survives at the heart of the present complex, in spite of many restorations and the often clumsy additions made by later monarchs.

Highlights of the Alcázar include the Chapel of the Navigators, where Isabella of Castile masterminded the conquest of the Spanish Americas. The room's coffered wooden ceiling, a classic example of *artesonado* style, is studded with golden stars. Inside the palace proper is the Patio of the Maidens, with fine stucco work and

azulejos tiling. Beyond lies the Salón de Carlos V, with another superb *artesonado* ceiling and then the Alcázar's finest room, the Salon of the Ambassadors, crowned by a glorious dome of wood in green, red and gold and with a Moorish arcade.

Adjoining the main palace are the dull and cavernous chambers of the Palacio de Carlos V, added by that insatiable intruder upon fine buildings, the Hapsburg king. These lead to the serene and lovely gardens of the Alcázar, where an arc of water from a high faucet crashes spectacularly into a pool in which a bronze statue of Mercury stands in front of a rusticated façade: the Gallery of the Grotesque. The rest of the gardens are a pleasant conclusion before you emerge into the Patio de las Banderas, with Seville's mighty cathedral beckoning ahead.

✚ *Sevilla 2b* ✉ Patio de las Banderas
☎ 954 50 23 23 🕔 Oct–Mar Tue–Sat 9:30–5, Sun 9:30–1:30; Apr–Oct Tue–Sat 9:30–7, Sun 9:30–5 ✋ Moderate; children under 12 and senior citizens free 🚌 C1, C2, C3, C4 ❓ A visit early or late in the day may win you some added space. At busier times, numbers are regulated and you may have to wait your turn
🛈 Avenida de la Constitución 21B
☎ 954 22 14 04; 954 21 81 57

Úbeda

Although famous for its Moorish architecture, Andalucía also boasts some of Spain's finest Renaissance buildings. Úbeda has some of the best.

Renaissance Úbeda survives triumphantly within its more modern and often featureless surroundings. To reach the crowning glory of the Plaza de Vázquez de Molina you need to navigate the urban maze from the town's modern centre at the busy Plaza de Andalucía. From here the narrow Calle Real runs gently downhill to the Plaza del Ayuntamiento, where a short street leads to the glorious enclave of Plaza de Vázquez de Molina. Just before entering the plaza, you will find, on the right, Úbeda's remarkable Museo de Alfarería (Pottery Museum).

On the right as you enter Plaza de Vázquez de Molina is the Palacio de las Cadenas, the work of the great classical architect Andrés Vandelvira. Directly opposite is the handsome Church of Santa María de los Reales Alcázares, enclosing a lovely Gothic cloister on the site of an original Moorish building. East of here lie other fine buildings, culminating in a 16th-century palace, now Úbeda's luxurious Parador hotel (➤ 93).

At the east end of the plaza is the Sacra Capilla del Salvador. This private burial chapel dates from the mid-16th century and was completed by Vandelvira to an earlier design. The grand exterior

apart, inside you will find a carefully restored *retablo* (altarpiece) of breathtaking splendour, beneath a soaring cupola. Other fine buildings and churches are found in Plaza San Pedro, reached from halfway down Calle Real, and in Plaza del Primero de Mayo, just north of Plaza de Vázquez de Molina.

➕ 12D ✉ 45km (28 miles) northeast of Jaén
🚌 Regular service Jaén–Úbeda, Granada–Úbeda,
Baeza–Úbeda ❓ *Fiesta de San Miguel*, 4 Oct
🛈 Palacio del Marqués del Contadero, c/ Bajo del
Marqués 4 ☎ 953 75 08 97

10 Zahara de la Sierra

Hailed as one of the finest of the *pueblos blancos* ('white towns') of Ronda, Zahara de la Sierra occupies a spectacular hilltop position, offering wonderful views.

The red-roofed, white-walled houses of the lovely village of Zahara cluster beneath a dramatic hilltop castle at the heart of the Sierra Margarita in the Parque Natural Sierra de Grazalema. Below, to the northeast, is a large reservoir, the Embalse de Zahara, formed by damming the Río Guadalete. Zahara's castle has Roman origins but was rebuilt by the Moors during the 12th century. It was later occupied by Christians, and its reckless retaking by the forces of Granada's Nasrid rulers in 1481 prompted Ferdinand and Isabella to launch the final conquest of Moorish Granada and its province.

If you visit Zahara by car, it is best to find a roadside parking space near the top of the steep approach road before entering the centre of the village. Zahara is a delightful hilltop enclave, its Moorish character intact. The castle has been recently renovated and is reached from the village square by following a winding pathway uphill past a charming cave fountain. The views from the castle and its tower are spectacular, but take care on the steep, unlit steps. The tiny village square stands in front of the baroque

church of Santa María de la Mesa and there is an airy *mirador*, a viewing balcony, overlooking the reservoir. At the other end of the main street, at the entrance to the village, is the little church of San Juan, which harbours some vivid statues. At night Zahara's castle is floodlit and its centre and side streets take on a charming intimacy.

✚ 15K ✉ 22km (14 miles) northwest of Ronda
🚌 Regular service Ronda–Zahara de la Sierra
❓ *Corpus Christi,* end May–early Jun
ℹ Plaza de la Rey 3 ☎ 956 12 31 14

Best things to do

Great places to have lunch	58–59
Best markets	60–61
Places to take the children	62–63
A walk through the Barrio Santa Cruz, Seville	64–65
Top activities	66–67
Stunning views	68–69
Beaches and resorts	70–71
Best buys	72–73

Great places to have lunch

Bar Giralda (€–€€)
One of the best tapas bars in Seville.
✉ Mateos Gago 1, Seville ☎ 954 22 74 35

Cádiz (€)
This pleasant little restaurant has an attractive courtyard for outdoor eating and offers good local dishes at reasonable prices. Game dishes when in season.
✉ Plaza España, Cádiz ☎ 956 41 02 50

El Chinitas (€)
Popular tapas bar and traditional restaurant offering regional dishes.
✉ c/ Moreno Monroy 4–6, Málaga ☎ 952 21 09 72

Gaitán (€€)
This prize-winning restaurant has a good reputation for quality cooking. The menu features traditional and nouvelle cuisine, with fish dishes a speciality.
✉ c/ Gaitán 3, Jerez ☎ 956 16 80 21

Mesón Diego (€)

Great local café-restaurant where you may even enjoy free tapas with your drinks before ordering a sit-down meal at the broad terrace, usually in the company of locals.

✉ Plaza Constitución 12, Alhama de Granada ☎ 958 36 01 21

El Molino (€–€€)

If you enjoy people-watching, head for El Molino, where you can sit on the terrace looking out on Ronda's busiest square. There's a good selection of main dishes and desserts.

✉ Plaza del Socorro 6, Ronda ☎ 952 87 93 32

La Parrala (€)

La Parrala is in a charming location on the gleaming white Plaza de las Monjas, alongside the walls of Moguer's Convento de Santa Clara. It's a popular gathering place for locals in the evenings.

✉ Plaza de las Monjas 22, Moguer ☎ 959 37 04 52

El Portalon (€€€)

This is one of the coast's top-notch restaurants. Choose from the excellent selection of fresh seafood dishes or opt for the delicious roast meats.

✉ Carretera Cádiz, Km 178, Marbella ☎ 952 86 10 75

Siena (€)

A well-placed café-restaurant for viewing life in Córdoba's Plaza de las Tendillas. It serves drinks, snacks and *platas combinados*.

✉ Plaza de las Tendillas, Córdoba ☎ 957 47 30 05

Vía Colón (€€)

Near the cathedral, Vía Colón has a pleasant outside terrace. Choose from a variety of snacks and local specialities.

✉ Gran Vía de Colón 13, Granada ☎ 958 22 98 42

Best markets

Almería: An exuberant morning food market is held in Calle Aguilar de Campo, daily.

Cádiz: There's a superb food market in La Libertad, Monday to Saturday mornings.

Carmona: The morning market is held in the arcaded patio of a 17th-century convent, south of Plaza de San Fernando.

Cazorla: You'll find local produce from the Sierras in the daily market in Plaza del Mercado.

Córdoba: A Saturday morning market in Plaza de Corderella sells general goods and has a marvellous atmosphere. The Zoco craft market, a re-creation of an Arab souk in the Judería, has stalls selling filigree silverwork.

Fuengirola: One of the largest markets on the Costa del Sol is the Tuesday morning market in Fuengirola, where anything from crafts to tomatoes is on sale.

Málaga: Join the locals at Málaga's morning market, the Mercado Atarazanas, west of Calle Marqués de Larios.

Órgiva: The western town of Las Alpujarras has a daily market with more than a hint of the 'alternative' culture introduced by northern European incomers.

Sanlúcar de Barrameda: This town, in Andalucía's sherry triangle, has a lively morning market in Calle Bretones, selling local specialities.

Seville: The jewellery and clothing market in the Plaza del Duque de la Victoria is held from Thursday to Saturday.

Places to take the children

Aqualand

Scores of popular water-based attractions, including huge slides, flumes, an artificial river, artificial waves, pools, and a Jacuzzi.
✉ c/ Cuba 10, Torremolinos ☎ 952 11 49 96; 952 38 88 88; www.aqualand.es ⏰ Mid-May to mid-Sep daily 10–6 🖐 Expensive

Crocodile Park

There are crocodiles large and small here. Watch them being fed, handle cuddly baby alligators and visit the 'Africa' museum.
✉ c/ Cuba 14, Torremolinos ☎ 952 05 17 82; www.crocodile-park.com
⏰ Mar–Jun, Oct, Nov daily 10–6; Jul–Sep 10–5 🖐 Moderate

Oasys

Once the location for Sergio Leone's famous 'Spaghetti Western' *A Fistful of Dollars*, this is now a full-blooded Western theme park. There are staged gunfights at High Noon and 5pm. There is also a safari wild animal park, the Reserva Zoológica, nearby.

✉ Carretera Nacional, Km 340, near Tabernas on the A370, Almería ☎ 950 36 52 36 (Oasys); 950 36 29 31 (Reserva Zoologica); www.oasysparquetematico.es

Parque Acuático Mijas

A big water fun park with endless pools, slides and flumes. Also on site is 'Aqualandia', a water play area for small children.
✉ Circunvalación, Km 290, Mijas Costa ☎ 952 46 04 04; www.aquamijas.com ⏰ May daily 10:30–5:30; Jun 10–6; Jul, Aug 10–7; Sep 10–6 🚌 Direct from Fuengirola bus terminal 🖐 Expensive

Parque de las Ciencias (Science Park)

Great fun and informative, the Science Park has ingenious interactive experiences, as well as an observatory and planetarium.

✉ Avenida del Mediterráneo s/n, Granada ☎ 958 13 19 00;
www.parqueciencias.com 🕐 Tue–Sat 10–7, Sun 10–3 🚍 5 👆 Moderate

Sea Life

A submarine view of Mediterranean sea life, from tiny shrimps and
shellfish to sharks. The feeding displays are always popular.

✉ Puerto Marina, Benalmádena Costa ☎ 952 56 01 50;
www.sealifeeurope.com 🕐 Daily 10–6 👆 Moderate

Selwo Aventura

A magnificent wild animal park where you can see such animals as
lions and elephants in their natural habitat.

✉ Autovía Costa del Sol, Km 162.5, Las Lomas del Monte, Estepona
☎ 902 19 04 82; www.selwo.es 🕐 Mon–Fri 10–6, Sun 10–7 👆 Expensive

Tivoli World

The ultimate Costa del Sol amusement park has been revamped.
There are funfair rides galore, a water flume, Wild West town,
open-air theatre, mock Spanish 'plaza' and live entertainment. It's
very popular during the summer and busy at weekends, especially.

✉ Avenida del Tivoli, Arroyo de la Miel, Benalmádena ☎ 952 57 70 16;
www.tivoli.es 🕐 Apr, May, mid-Sep to Oct 4pm–1am; Jun, early Sep
5pm–2am; Jul, Aug 6pm–3am; Nov–Mar 11am–9pm 👆 Moderate

Whales and Dolphins

Go whale- and dolphin-spotting from fast boats in the Strait of
Gibraltar. It's an exciting day out, even though a glimpse of these
fine creatures is not guaranteed. Companies running trips include:
FIRMM ✉ c/ Pedro Cortés 4, Tarifa ☎ 956 62 70 08; www.firmm.org
Whale Watch Tarifa ✉ Avenida de la Constitución 6, Tarifa
☎ 956 62 70 13; www.whalewatchtarifa.net 👆 Expensive

Zoo Fuengirola

A great zoo where numerous species of animals and birds can be
seen in their natural habitat.

✉ Camilo José Cela, Fuengirola ☎ 952 66 63 01; www.zoofuengirola.com
🕐 Daily 10–6 (Jul, Aug 10am–midnight) 👆 Moderate

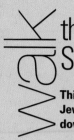

a walk through the Barrio Santa Cruz, Seville

This is a tour of the Barrio's old Jewish quarter; you can divert at will down numerous alleyways on the way.

From Plaza Virgen de los Reyes walk up Calle Mateos Gago and at the junction go right down Mesón del Moro. At the junction with Ximenez de Encisco go left, then right down Cruces to a small square.

At the centre of the square are three slightly incongruous columns, the most conspicuous survivors of Roman Seville.

Leave the square by its left-hand corner and go down Mariscal into Plaza de Refinadores. (You can divert into the pleasant Jardines de Murillo here.) Go right, across the back of the plaza, then down Mezquita into Plaza de Santa Cruz.

Just off Plaza de Santa Cruz is Calle Santa Teresa. The Museo de Murillo at No 8 traces the life of painter Bartolomé Esteban Murillo (1617–82), who lived here.

Leave the Plaza de Santa Cruz by its left-hand corner and enter the Plaza Alfaro. Go right along Lope de Rueda, then right to reach Reinosa. Go left, then left again at Jamerdana to the Plaza de los Venerables.

There are guided tours (daily 10–2, 4–8) of the Hospicio de los Venerables Sacerdotes, which has a marvellous patio and superb paintings.

Leave the plaza along Calle Gloria to reach the Plaza Doña Elvira. Leave by the Vida and go into the Judería. Turn right, then go through vaulted archways to Patio de las Banderas. Cross the square and go under the archway to the Plaza del Triunfo and the Gothic cathedral.

Distance 1.5km (1 mile)
Time About 3 hours, with visits to museums
Start/End point Plaza Virgen de los Reyes
✚ *Sevilla 2b*
Lunch Hostería del Laurel (€€) ✉ Plaza de los Venerables 5
☎ 954 22 02 95

Top activities

Bird-watching: In spite of widespread shooting and other hazards, birds flock in and out of coastal Andalucía, especially in spring and autumn. The coastal nature parks are the places to be.

Football match: If there is a big match on, especially in somewhere like Málaga, go along for the fantastic atmosphere.

Horse-riding: In the land of great horse-handling and riding, what else should you do?

Mountain biking: The Sierra Nevada has become one of the leading mountain-biking destinations in Europe.

People-watching: The ultimate activity. Choose a good café in a busy plaza or village square, morning or evening.

Scuba-diving: Andalucía under water can be as spectacular as it is on land. Diving courses are available at various resorts.

Sightseeing: Everywhere, you will be spoiled for choice.

Swimming: The entire coast of Andalucía is yours to choose from, but look out also for village and local swimming pools deep inland. They can be a great way to cool off.

Tennis and golf: The Costa del Sol is the place for these sports. There are numerous courts and courses, although you may need to book well ahead and join a queue.

Walking: This is a rather non-Andalucían habit. But in the mountains, or along the more remote coastline, it is a glorious way of enjoying the countryside.

Windsurfing: Head for the Tarifa coastline of the Costa de la Luz for some of the best windsurfing conditions in the world.

Stunning views

Granada's Alhambra from the Mirador de San Nicolás (➤ 109).

Cazorla's ruined castle, La Yedra (➤ 84), from the town centre's outer wall, as swifts and swallows wheel about the sky.

The windsurfers at Tarifa beach (➤ 149), as they speed along the windiest stretch of sea in Andalucía and soar above the waves.

The hill country surrounding the town of Priego de Córdoba, best viewed from the old town (➤ 48–49).

Mulhacén, Spain's highest peak, from the A348 as you drive through the Alpujarras (➤ 116–117).

The interior of La Mezquita. Nowhere in Andalucía is the Moorish legacy so beautiful and expressive as inside Córdoba's mosque, where 1,200 columns support the building's arches (➤ 44–45).

A flamenco bar in Seville in full swing. See this passionate dance performed in one of Seville's venues (➤ 185).

Beaches and resorts

Costa del Sol

Overpopulated by sunseekers and overshadowed by high-rise apartment blocks, the Costa del Sol (➤ 144) isn't the most promising place to seek beautiful beaches and resorts. However, several of the resorts have survived the beachfront developments with some local character intact. Chief among these is **Estepona,** an upscale resort to the west of the Costa del Sol. It has a fine, clean beach and an appealing promenade, which becomes very busy on summer evenings.

The next resort of interest, sidestepping several concrete jungles, is **Marbella,** where the Mediterranean jetset flashes its cash (although the celebrities moved on years ago). This is a land of luxury apartments, vast yachts and an expensive nightlife. The best resort east of Málaga is **Nerja** (▶ 147). The Balcón de Europa here overlooks the small, quiet beach.

Almería and Granada

The main resort in Almería is **Mojácar** (▶ 115), where the long sandy beach is the best feature, although it gets busy in the height of summer. In Granada province, on what is known as the Costa Tropical (▶ 114), head for the resorts of **Almuñécar** and **Salobreña** for the best beaches. Almuñécar is a low-key but attractive resort with some Moorish ruins.

Costa de la Luz

The beaches around **Cádiz** (▶ 139) are pounded by Atlantic rollers and high winds – they're popular with active types and those seeking more space. The best beaches here are the golden Los Caños de Meca and Zahara de los Atunes' stretches of sand. Windsurfers and kitesurfers flock to **Tarifa** (▶ 149): the southern tip of Spain has some of the world's most demanding conditions for the sports.

Nature reserves

If you prefer bird-watching to sunbathing, the coastal nature reserves of **Parque Nacional de Doñana,** to the far west of Andalucía, and **Cabo de Gata** at the eastern end of Andalucía, see many wetland species flying in during the year.

Best buys

Jamón serrano, the air-dried ham from Trevélez and other villages in the Alpujarras (➤ 129). The hams are hung for up to two years. In addition to *jamón serrano* there are other regional hams, differing according to the breed of pig, what the animal has been fed on and how the meat has been cured. To the west, in Aracena province, *jamón ibérico* will feature more on tapas menus. *Jamón ibérico* is produced in the Sierra de Aracena from pigs fed on acorns.

Olive oil from Cazorla (➤ 99).

Ceramic tiles or pots from Nijar, Sorbas, Úbeda or Seville. Úbeda's ceramics (➤ 98) are particularly distinctive, being finished in a traditional green glaze introduced by the Moors.

Esparto ware from Úbeda. Craft shops sell traditional items made from this coarse grass.

Fino **sherry** (➤ 14) from Jerez de la Frontera or Sanlúcar de Barrameda. Discover the difference between dry, delicate *fino* and sweet, toffee-coloured *Moscatel* in one of the many bodegas in Jerez. The tourist office even organises tasting routes around the region. Sherry: an old ladies' drink? Certainly not. You'll never look at sherry in the same way again.

Flamenco costume and accessories from Seville (➤ 184).

Honey or pears in wine from Grazalema (➤ 160).

Seafood in Cádiz. This port's fishermen may be struggling, but the city's Mercado Central can still be relied upon to sell startlingly fresh fish and seafood. Among the chunks of tuna and swordfish, look for the local *chorizo carabineros* – huge pink prawns. Stalls will fry whitebait on the spot for you.

Exploring

Córdoba and Jaén Provinces   77–100

Granada and Almería Provinces   101–130

Málaga and Cádiz Provinces   131–164

Seville and Huelva Provinces   165–185

Sunseeker, sightseer, foodie: whatever you love, Andalucía will get your heart racing. It's a thrillingly varied, beautiful region of Spain, drenched in sunlight for most of the year. Yes, parts have become stale with resort developments, but that's all the more reason to explore the enthralling interior, where you'll receive a warm welcome, and perhaps a chilled glass of *fino*.

The Moors conquered this southern area of Spain, which extends from the pounding surf of the Atlantic to the green rolling hills of Jerez, eastward to the mountains of the Sierra Nevada, in a couple of centuries. They left their mark in a series of buildings – from Granada's Alhambra to Córdoba's Mezquita – that are wonders of the Islamic world. Andalucían cities are among Spain's most vibrant, with Seville and Córdoba leading the nation in flamenco and tapas. Cádiz has an air of faded glamour, while Jerez is famous for sherry.

Córdoba and Jaén Provinces

The provinces of Córdoba and Jaén are where Moorish and Renaissance Spain overlap and where a more northern European influence has imposed itself on Mediterranean Andalucía.

The Río (river) Guadalquivir neatly divides Córdoba province, and the city of Córdoba stands on its northern banks. To the north and

west lie the smooth, wooded hills of the Sierra Morena; south is the farming country of the Campiña, dotted with olives and vines and patched with fields of golden grain. Here lie delightful towns and villages such as Priego de Córdoba and Zuheros.

The city of Jaén and its nearby towns of Baeza and Úbeda are more Renaissance than Moorish. They sit at the centre of Jaén province, a landscape of regimented olive trees (these have provided Jaén's staple product for centuries), where low hills extend towards the dramatic mountain wall of the Sierra Cazorla in the east.

CÓRDOBA

The city of Córdoba has a spectacular past. In 152BC the Romans founded their settlement of *Corduba* on the banks of the Río Guadalquivir, and for six centuries the city flourished, enriched by trade in olive oil, minerals and wool. Moorish conquest in the 8th century eventually made Córdoba a glittering rival to Baghdad as a centre of Islamic culture.

Modern Córdoba is a small city with a big heart. It has an engaging intimacy not found in Granada or Seville and is less traffic-bound than these main urban centres. The pedestrianized central areas merge satisfyingly with the narrow streets of the Judería, the old quarter that encloses the Mezquita (► 44–45), Córdoba's world-renowned mosque, a breathtaking survivor of Moorish Andalucía. In hidden corners of the city, away from the crowded areas, you will feel the engaging spirit of an older Spain.

A visit to the ruins of the 10th-century palace of **Medina Azahara,** a few kilometres outside the city, gives some perspective on Córdoba's importance during the Moorish period. In the 11th century the Christian Reconquest signalled the beginning of the city's decline, until 20th-century agriculture, light industry and tourism shaped the flourishing Córdoba of today.

This city has great style, which is reflected in its mix of lively bars and top-quality restaurants, and in its fashionable shops. The happy merging of the past with the present is what makes Córdoba so appealing.

✚ 8D 🛈 c/ Torrijos 10 ☎ 957 47 12 35
❓ *Fiesta de los Patios*, early May

Medina Azahara

✉ 7km (4 miles) west of Córdoba, on the CP199 off the A431 ☎ 957 32 91 30
🕐 Tue–Sat and Sun mornings 💷 Inexpensive; free with EU passport

Alcázar de los Reyes Cristianos

Córdoba's Alcázar de los Reyes Cristianos (Palace of the Christian Kings) is an interesting hybrid of Christian and Moorish features that epitomise the Mudéjar architectural styles of medieval Andalucía. It was built during the late 13th century, soon after the Reconquest, as a palace for the Christian monarchs. The building houses a museum in which there are some outstanding Roman mosaics. The gardens are real sun traps and blaze with colourful flowerbeds and shrubs, while ponds and fountains glitter in the unforgiving sunlight. Cool interiors compensate for the heat.

✉ Plaza Campo Santo de los Mártires ☎ 957 42 01 51 ⏰ Tue–Sat 10–2, 4:30–7:30; Sun 9:30–2:30 ✋ Moderate; free Tue 🍴 Bar-Restaurante Millán, Avenida Dr Fleming 14 (€€)

Judería

The engaging maze of narrow alleys that lies between the Plaza Tendillas and the Mezquita is the Judería, Córdoba's old Jewish quarter. The area of the Judería close to the Mezquita is given over to souvenir shops, but there is still much charm in popular venues such as the flower-bedecked Callejón de las Flores, a narrow cul-de-sac whose walls neatly frame the Mezquita's old minaret tower. At Calle Maimónides 18, near the Museum of Bullfighting, there is a 14th-century synagogue, the only one in Andalucía and a good example of Mudéjar architecture. Near the synagogue is the Puerta de Almodóvar, a 14th-century city gate flanked by a statue of the Roman scholar Seneca, who was born in the Judería.

La Mezquita

Best places to see, ➤ 44–45.

Museo Arqueológico Provincial

Córdoba's Archaeological Museum occupies a delightful Renaissance mansion, the Palacio de los Páez. The arcaded entrance patio (a well-known Córdoban feature), along with the building's coffered ceilings and elegant staircases, enhances the excellent displays of prehistoric, Roman and Moorish exhibits. These include Roman mosaics and tombstones, and a Moorish bronze in the form of a stag, found at the ruins of Medina Azahara.

✉ Plaza Jerónimo Páez ☎ 957 35 55 17 🕐 Tue 2:30–8:30, Wed–Sat 9–8:30, Sun 9–2:30 ♨ Inexpensive; free with EU passport
🍽 Several cafés (€–€€€)

More to see in Córdoba and Jaén Provinces

BAEZA

Renaissance elegance is the hallmark of Baeza's old quarter, where remnants of long years of Moorish influence have been replaced with 16th-century classical buildings of the highest order. The busy, central Plaza de España extends into the tree-lined Paseo de la Constitución, with its lively pavement bars and cafés. The town's Renaissance treasures lie on the higher ground, east of here. At the southern end of the Paseo de la Constitución is the handsome Plaza de los Leones, also known as Plaza del Pópulo, with its fountain and double-arched gateway, the Puerta de Jaén.

Steps (Escalerillas de la Audienca) lead from the tourist office, then left to Plaza Santa Cruz, where you will find the Palace of Jabalquinto, with its superbly ornamented Gothic façade. The Renaissance courtyard and glorious baroque staircase are in poor condition, but are being refurbished. Opposite the palace is the

delightful little Romanesque church of Santa Cruz, with traces of the earlier mosque that it supplanted.

The Cuesta de San Felipe leads uphill from Plaza Santa Cruz to Plaza de Santa María, the magnificent heart of Renaissance Baeza. The plaza is dominated by Baeza's massive 13th-century cathedral, which has an exhilarating 16th-century nave. At the centre of the square is a fountain in the form of a rustic triumphal arch, behind which stands the 16th-century seminary of San Felipe Neri, its walls bearing elegant graffiti.

➕ 11D ✉ 48km (30 miles) northeast of Jaén 🚍 Regular services Jaén–Baeza, Granada–Baeza, Úbeda–Baeza 🚉 Railway station at Linares-Baeza, 14km (9 miles) from Baeza; connecting buses ❓ *Semana Santa* (Holy Week), Mar/Apr; *Romería del Cristo de la Yedra*, 7 Sep
ℹ️ Plaza del Pópulo s/n ☎ 953 74 04 44

BAÑOS DE LA ENCINA

This engaging hilltop village rises from acres of olive fields. It is dominated by its well-preserved, 10th-century Moorish castle. The custodian may be at the airy *mirador* on the way up to the castle; if not, ask at the Town Hall. You will be ushered through the double horseshoe arch into a huge central keep, where you can climb the Tower of Homage. Take care on the dark stairways: pigeons often explode into the light, and you may find their eggs perched mid-step. The views from the top are magnificent. Resist the challenge to walk round the inner, unprotected parapet if you do not have good footwork.

➕ 11D ✉ 100km (62 miles) east of Córdoba 🚍 Regular services Córdoba–Bailén, Úbeda–Bailén; local bus connections between Bailén and Baños ℹ️ Avenida José Luís Messias 2 ☎ 953 613 266

CAZORLA

The busy, unpretentious town of Cazorla nestles below the looming cliffs of the Peña de los Halcones. There is a lively daily market in Plaza del Mercado between the car park and Calle Dr Muñoz, the main shopping street. Plaza de la Corredera, Cazorla's more sedate square, is surrounded by cafés and shops. From its far right-hand corner the narrow Calle Nubla leads past the superb viewpoint of Balcón del Pintor Zabaleta, for views of Cazorla's ruined Moorish castle, La Yedra, and its ruined Renaissance church of Santa María. Ruination apart, Plaza Santa María, below the church, is a wonderful place to eat and drink.

The town is gateway to the Parque Natural de Cazorla, Segura y Las Villas, a marvellous area of mountains and forests, where the Guadalquivir river has its source (➤ 88).

✚ 12E ✉ 32km (20 miles) southeast of Úbeda

🚌 Regular services Granada–Cazorla, Jaén–Cazorla, Úbeda–Cazorla

❓ Pilgrimage to La Virgen de la Cabeza, last Sun/Mon in Apr

ℹ Paseo del Santo Cristo 17 ☎ 953 71 01 02; c/ Hilario Marco; Parque Natural Information Centre, c/ Martínez Falero 11 ☎ 953 71 15 34

JAÉN

Jaén is often given short shrift in terms of its appeal to the visitor. It is a pleasant enough city, however, though not as exotically Andalucían as other centres. Moorish moods still prevail in the old quarters of La Magdalena and San Juan, on the northeastern slopes of the Hill of Santa Catalina, and exploration of their streets is rewarding.

The scrub-covered Hill of Santa Catalina is crowned by the Castillo de Santa Catalina, its remnants transformed into a

luxurious *parador* (state-run hotel). It is a stiff hike to the top of the hill, but the view from the cross-crowned *mirador* near the southern ruins is spectacular.

Down at street level, Jaén's main attraction is its vast and magnificent 16th-century cathedral. The west façade is a fine example of Renaissance baroque. The gloomy interior has an impressive display of fluted Corinthian columns and rich carving. Other fine sights in Jaén include the Baños Árabes (Arab Baths), in the basement of the arts and crafts museum at the 16th-century Palacio de Villadompardo, just off Plaza San Blas. Another worthwhile visit can be made to the Museo Provincial in Paseo de la Estación. Collections from prehistory to Moorish and Renaissance times vie with the Museo de Bellas Artes (Museum of Fine Arts) upstairs, where there are some spectacularly bad but entertaining paintings, with provocative nudes in abundance.

www.andalucia.org

✚ 10E ✉ 90km (56 miles) east of Córdoba

🚆 Paseo de la Estación ☎ 902 24 02 02

🚌 Plaza Coca de la Piñera ☎ 953 25 01 06

❓ *Semana Santa* (Holy Week), Mar/Apr; San Lucas Fair, mid-Oct

🛈 c/ de la Maestra 13 ☎ 953 31 32 81

PRIEGO DE CÓRDOBA

Best places to see, ➤ 48–49.

a drive through the Sierras

This is quite a long drive, with a great deal to see. An overnight stop at somewhere like Segura de la Sierra is worthwhile.

From Úbeda go east along the N322, signed Valencia, Albacete. After 2km (1.25 miles), bear right, signed Cazorla. Watch carefully for a 'Halt' sign and at a roundabout, take the exit signed A315, Cazorla.

The road winds pleasantly towards distant mountains through low hills covered with olive trees. Fields of wheat and barley shine like gold in early summer.

At the main square of Cazorla (▶ 84) go round the roundabout and take the higher road marked 'Sierra' on its surface and signed for Parque Natural. Pass La Iruela village, where a ruined castle stands on a rock pinnacle. At Burunchal take the right fork, signed Parque Natural. Follow the winding A319 through magnificent scenery. After 15km (9 miles), go left at a junction signed Coto Ríos (or for a walk, ▶ 90–91).

The road follows the Guadalquivir valley through beautiful wooded mountains, passes the visitors' centre at Torre del Vinagre, then runs alongside the Tranco reservoir.

Two thirds of the way along the reservoir, cross a dam and keep right at the junction. After 9km (5.5 miles), at a junction below the hilltop village of Hornos, go left, signed

Cortijos Nuevos. Go through Cortijos and at roundabout take second right, signed La Puerta de Segura. Continue on the A317 and follow signs for Puerta de Segura and Albacete. Drive carefully through Puerta de Segura, then follow signs for Puente Génave and Úbeda. Join the N322 and return to Úbeda.

Distance 214km (133 miles)
Time 8 hours
Start/End point Úbeda ✚ 12D
Lunch Café de la Corredera (€) ✉ Plaza de la Corredera, Cazorla

SIERRAS DE CAZORLA, SEGURA Y LAS VILLAS

The Sierras of Cazorla, Segura and Las Villas make up the largest of Andalucía's Parque Naturales (Natural Parks) at an impressive 214,000ha (530,000 acres). The Sierras are a complex of deep valleys and high ridges, with the mountain of Las Empanadas being the highest point at 2,107m (6,910ft). This is a winter landscape of snow and ice, but in late spring, summer and autumn the Sierras are delightful, often hot and sunny, yet verdant, with higher than average rainfall for such terrain. There are good opportunities for short or long walks, and you can also book trips on off-road Land Rovers. More than 1,000 plant species include the Cazorla violet, unique to the area. Trees include the black pine, Aleppo pine and evergreen oaks, and there is a multitude of animals large and small, including fox, wild cat, polecat, otter, deer, mountain goat and wild boar. Birds include griffon vulture, booted and golden eagles, peregrine falcon and kite.

At Torre del Vinagre, 34km (21 miles) northeast of Cazorla, there is an **interpretation centre**, where you can book Land Rover trips and mountain bike or horse rides.

✚ 23H ✉ 90km (56 miles) northeast of Jaén 🍴 Bars, cafés and restaurants (€–€€) 🚌 Twice daily Cazorla–Torre del Vinagre–Cotos Ríos ❗ Parque Natural Information Centre, c/ Martinez Falero 11, Cazorla ☎ 953 71 15 34

Centro de Interpretación Torre del Vinagre

✉ Torre del Vinagre ☎ 953 71 30 17 🕐 Summer daily 10–2, 5–8:30; spring and autumn daily 11–2, 4–7:30; winter Tue–Sun 11–2, 4–5:30

SEGURA DE LA SIERRA

It is a challenging piece of tortuous driving to reach this charming village, which perches on a 1,100m (3,600ft) hill surrounded by peaks. You enter the village through a medieval gateway. Below the tiny square of Plaza de la Encomienda is the Iglesia Nuestra Señora del Collado, a handsome little church with tiled roof and simple interior. Opposite the church is a superb Renaissance

fountain, the Fuente Carlos V. Near the church is a well-preserved Arab bath house.

Segura's castle has been much renovated over the years. You may need to ask for the key at the tourist office, but the gate is often open – a reward for the stiff climb past the Plaza de Toros, Segura's tiny bullring. During the October festival there is a *corrida* (bullfight) here; famous matadors, such as Enrique Ponce, have fought here. The view from the castle tower is outstanding, but take care on the dark stairways.

🚹 23G 🖂 60km (37 miles) northeast of Úbeda 🍽 Casa Mesón Jorge Manríque (€€) 🚸 *Santa Quiteria*, 22 May; *Santiago*, 25 Jul; *Virgen del Rosario*, 5–8 Oct 🛈 c/ Regidor Juan de Isla, 1 ☎ 953 48 07 84

ÚBEDA

Best places to see, ➤ 52–53.

ZUHEROS

The white houses of Zuheros cluster below a Moorish castle in the Sierra Subbética, in a world of cliffs and rocky bluffs. The village has a handsome church, the Iglesia de la Virgen de los Remedios, whose tower supplanted an earlier minaret. The narrow streets are punctuated by fine viewpoints such as the Mirador de la Villa. East of Zuheros is the Cueva de los Murciélagos (Cave of the Bats), with prehistoric paintings (with guided tours at weekends).

🚹 19H 🖂 60km (37 miles) southeast of Córdoba 🍽 Mesón Atalaya, c/ Santo 58 (€) 🛈 Plaza de le Paz 2 ☎ 957 69 45 45

a walk along the Guadalquivir

A short walk through dramatic mountain scenery alongside the infant Río Guadalquivir.

From the parking space, walk downhill to reach a bridge over the Río Guadalquivir. Don't cross the bridge but turn left along a rocky path.

The Guadalquivir was named Guad al Quivir (Great River) by the Moors. It rises in the heart of the Sierra de Cazorla and flows through Andalucía for 657km (407 miles) to the sea at Sanlúcar de Barrameda.

Follow the rocky path as it rises along the side of the river valley. Descend steeply and go down winding steps to reach a weir. Go down steps to the base of a waterfall that drops from the weir.

The valley widens here and is flanked by great cliffs. Dragonflies and damselflies flit across the river pools.

Continue along the path beneath overhanging cliffs. There are shaded seats alongside the path.

Swifts dip and weave through the sky from their nests in the looming rocks above. Keep an eye open for mountain goats, which often graze at these lower levels.

Soon the path leads above a deep wooded valley and reaches a superb viewpoint just beyond an old well head and water pipe. Continue along a track through trees and keep left on the main track. At the next junction go right to reach a road and large parking area beside a notice board. Turn left and go downhill for a short distance to the parking space.

Distance 2km (1.25 miles)

Time 1 hour

Start/end point Follow instructions for the Sierras drive (► 86–87) to the turning at the junction signed Coto Ríos; keep right here, signed Parador de Turismo. There's a café and seating at the base of the hill. The road worsens here noticeably. At the next junction keep left, signed Vadillo Castril. Soon, at a wide area, reach a junction with a road bending sharply right. Keep ahead for about 100m (110 yards) to a parking space on the right, just before a small house ✚ 22H

Lunch Parador de Cazorla (€€€) ✉ Sierra de Cazorla s/n ☎ 953 72 70 75

HOTELS

BAEZA

Hospedería Fuentenueva (€€)

Charming 12-bedroom hotel, once a prison – now transformed by sophisticated décor and furnishings. Regular art exhibitions. Excellent restaurant.

✉ Avenida Puche Pardo s/n ☎ 953 74 31 00; www.fuentenueva.com

CAZORLA

Hotel Guadalquivir (€€)

A pleasant hotel located at the heart of the town, between Plaza Corredera and Plaza Santa María.

✉ c/ Nueva 6 ☎ 953 72 02 68; www.hguadalquivir.com

CÓRDOBA

Hospedería de El Churrasco (€€)

Conveniently located next to the restaurant of the same name (► 94) in the heart of the Judería, El Churrasco is a small but smart boutique hotel with individually decorated rooms.

✉ Romero 38 ☎ 957 29 48 08; www.elchurrasco.com

Hotel Maestre (€)

Smart, modern hotel with bright and airy patios. Adjoining is the slightly cheaper Hostal Maestre, under the same management. The company also has apartments to let.

✉ c/ Romero Barros 4–6 ☎ 957 47 24 10; www.hotelmaestre.com

Hotel Mezquita (€€)

Conveniently located opposite the mosque, this 16th-century mansion is restored in Spanish style, with a charming courtyard.

✉ Plaza Santa Catalina ☎ 957 47 55 85

Hotel Los Omeyas (€€)

Located in the heart of the Judería, the old quarter of the city, only a few steps from the Mezquita and other attractions. Arab motifs throughout, including a traditional courtyard patio.

✉ c/ Encarnación 17 ☎ 957 49 22 67/21 27

NH Amistad Córdoba (€€€)

The stylish NH Amistad is close La Mezquita and other key sights of the old town, but it has its own parking area. The 18th-century exterior hides a contemporary interior.

✉ Plaza Maimonides 3 ☎ 957 42 03 35; www.nh-hoteles.com

JAÉN

Hotel Xauen (€€)

Just off the Plaza de la Constitución. Rooms have air-conditioning. Self-service coffee shop. Parking.

✉ Plaza de Deán Mazas 3 ☎ 953 24 07 89; www.hotelxauenjaen.com

PRIEGO DE CÓRDOBA

Hostal Rafi (€)

At the bottom end of the price range, this delightful *hostal* lies in a narrow street near the Plaza de la Constitución.

✉ Isabel la Católica 4 ☎ 957 54 07 49; www.hostalrafi.net

SEGURA DE LA SIERRA

Los Huertos de Segura (€€)

At the village's highest point, with apartments for 2 to 4 people, with bathroom, kitchenette, open fireplace and magnificent views. Welcoming atmosphere. Restaurant close by.

✉ c/ Castillo 11 ☎ 953 48 04 02; www.loshuertosdesegura.com

ÚBEDA

Parador de Úbeda (€€)

Charming location in the handsome Plaza de Vázquez de Molina. Originally a 16th-century palace, the *parador* retains many period features, including an inner courtyard with galleries.

✉ Plaza de Vázquez Molina s/n ☎ 953 75 03 45; www.parador.es

ZUHEROS

Hotel Zuhayra (€€)

Delightful little hotel with its own pool and patio. Tasty local dishes in the restaurant.

✉ c/ Mirador 10 ☎ 957 69 46 93

RESTAURANTS

CÓRDOBA

El Caballo Rojo (€€€)

Excellent Córdoban cuisine at this famous restaurant, frequented by royalty when they're in town. Specializes in classic local dishes.

✉ Cardenal Herrero 28 ☎ 957 47 53 75 🕓 Lunch and dinner

Los Califas (€€)

Attractive restaurant in the old quarter and with a rooftop terrace. Specializes in Córdoban regional cuisine, with good meat dishes.

✉ c/ Deanes 3 ☎ 957 47 13 20 🕓 Lunch and dinner

El Churrasco (€€)

Andalucían cuisine at its finest. It's at the top end of the price range for special dishes, but with reasonable set menu otherwise.

✉ c/ Romero 16 ☎ 957 29 08 19 🕓 Lunch and dinner. Closed Aug

Pizzaiolo (€)

Well-run pizzeria in an attractive square. Features proudly in the *Guinness Book of Records* as having 360 different toppings.

✉ Calle San Felipe 5 ☎ 957 48 64 33 🕓 Lunch and dinner

Siena (€)

See page 59.

Taberna San Miguel (€)

One of Córdoba's most popular establishments, with a lively ambience and a wide selection of tapas.

✉ Plaza San Miguel 1 ☎ 957 47 83 28 🕓 Lunch and dinner

BAEZA

Casa Juanito (€€)

Tasty and unusual dishes based on traditional recipes. Specialities include partridge salad, fillet of beef with tomatoes and peppers, and artichoke hearts with tomatoes and garlic.

✉ Avenida Arca del Agua ☎ 953 74 00 40 🕓 Lunch and dinner. Closed dinner Sun and Mon

La Góndola (€)

Cosy local bar and restaurant with a brick and tile interior and an open fireplace. Tapas include the tasty speciality *patatas baezanas*, sautéed potatoes topped with fried mushrooms, parsley and garlic.

✉ Portales Carboneria 13 ☎ 953 74 29 84 🕐 Lunch and dinner

CAZORLA

Café de la Corredera (€)

Serving breakfast, lunch and dinner, this café in Cazorla's new square has a tempting range of international beers in addition to its tasty food.

✉ Plaza de la Corredera ☎ 953 72 01 02 🕐 Breakfast, lunch and dinner

Juan Carlos (€–€€)

Popular restaurant in the centre of town serving a wide choice of interesting game dishes, as well as some innovative starters, such as cream of melon soup with mint. Excellent desserts, including home-made fig ice cream.

✉ Plaza Consuela Mendieta 2 ☎ 953 72 12 01 🕐 Lunch and dinner

Parador de Cazorla (€€€)

Making your way along forested mountain roads to this quality restaurant, part of Cazorla's *parador*, is a fine preparation for good Sierra cuisine, including *gachamiga*, a tasty bacon dish. Reservations advised for non-residents.

✉ Sierra Cazorla s/n ☎ 953 72 70 75 🕐 Lunch and dinner

La Sarga (€€–€€€)

Cazorla's most refined dining experience comes in the unlikely form of La Sarga, a restaurant where chef José Polaina transforms rustic meals for mountain people into rustic meals for fine diners. The wine list has a fantastic selection of local wines at generous prices.

✉ Plaza del Mercado 2 ☎ 953 72 15 07; www.lasarga.com 🕐 Lunch and dinner. Closed Tue

JAÉN

Bar La Vina (€€)

On a small street close to the cathedral, this dressy tapas bar pulls a loyal lunchtime crowd. There are several good bars and restaurants on this street. For meals, local specialities include scrambled eggs with eel, but whatever you choose, note that the portions are large.

✉ c/ Maestra 8 ☎ 953 23 96 60 🕓 Mon–Thu lunch and dinner, Fri, Sat dinner only. Closed Sun pm

Casa Vicente (€€€)

Top Jaén eating place, housed in a restored palace near the cathedral. Excellent local cuisine with game specialities.

✉ c/ Francisco Marín Mora 1 ☎ 953 23 22 22 🕓 Lunch and dinner. Closed Sun dinner and Aug

Parador de Jaén (€€)

High-quality cuisine in high surroundings at the restaurant of Jaén's Moorish *parador*. Andalucían specialities such as the famous *morcilla en caldera* (blood sausage), served in mock-medieval surroundings. Reservations advised for non-residents.

✉ Castillo de Santa Catalina ☎ 953 23 00 00 🕓 Lunch and dinner

PRIEGO DE CÓRDOBA

El Aljibe (€–€€)

Friendly tapas bar and restaurant opposite the stunning Iglesia de la Asunción, serving unusual local dishes such as dates stuffed with bacon. More formal restaurant downstairs with a reasonably priced *menu del día*.

✉ c/ Abad Palomino 7 ☎ 957 70 18 56 🕓 Lunch and dinner. Closed Mon

La Noria (€€)

Enjoying one of best locations in town, the sunny side of the Abad Palomino square, La Noria is a great spot for a light lunch or drink. The menu ranges from salads to roasted pork.

✉ Abad Palomino 18 ☎ 957 54 27 27; www.epriego.com/lanoria
🕓 Lunch and dinner

Rafi (€)

Part of the Hostal Rafi, this relaxed restaurant has tasty local dishes served in a cheerful atmosphere and often in the company of friendly locals.

✉ c/ Isabel la Catolica 4 ☎ 957 54 07 49 🕔 Lunch and dinner. Closed Mon

SEGURA DE LA SIERRA

Bar Peralta (€)

Located on the way up to the entrance arch to the upper town, this local bar serves tapas and *raciones* and does tasty plate-loads of pork crackling.

✉ c/ Regidor Juan de Isla 12 ☎ No phone 🕔 Lunch and dinner

ÚBEDA

El Gallo Rojo (€)

You'll get good value at this popular restaurant to the north of Plaza de Andalucía. Regional dishes can be enjoyed at outside tables, a reasonable distance from a busy junction. Reservations are advised.

✉ c/ Manuel Barraca 3 ☎ 953 75 20 38 🕔 Lunch and dinner

Mesón Barbacoa (€)

This is an intriguing restaurant-cum-agricultural museum. The walls are crammed with farming implements and the rafters hung with traditional bags, baskets and containers. There's a good selection of *platos combinados* to go with the rustic décor.

✉ c/ San Cristobal 17 ☎ 953 79 04 73 🕔 Lunch and dinner

ZUHEROS

Restaurant Zuhayra (€€)

Located in the hotel of the same name, this restaurant has a good selection of local dishes, often flavoured with the area's famous olive oil. You can also enjoy Córdoba province's equally renowned *montilla* wine, which should be a compulsory accompaniment to the meal.

✉ c/ Mirador 10 ☎ 957 69 46 93 🕔 Lunch and dinner

SHOPPING

ARTS, CRAFTS, GIFTS AND ANTIQUES

Alfarería Gongora

This well-known potter has his shop in the 'street of potters' in
Úbeda – a town famous for its attractive dark green pottery.

✉ c/ Cuesta de la Merced 32, Úbeda ☎ 953 75 46 05

Alfarería Tito

This shop in Úbeda's old town showcases the work of the Tito
family, with Islamic-inspired vases and Andalucían glazes
replicating the region's 16th-century pottery. Expect to pay top
dollar, but the quality is unmistakable.

✉ Plaza del Ayuntamiento 12, Úbeda ☎ 953 75 13 02

Baraka

The work of Córdoban artists is showcased at this arts and crafts
shop in the Judería. Prices reflect the touristy location.

✉ Deanes, Manríquez s/n, Córdoba ☎ 957 48 83 27

Meryan

Córdoba was once famed for its leatherwork – as evidenced by the
new museum, Casa Museo Arte Sobre Piel, on Plaza de
Agrupación de Cofradías. This shop is one of the few places where
you can still buy traditional Cordoban leatherwork.

✉ Calleja de las Flores, 2, Córdoba ☎ 957 47 59 02; www.meryancor.com

El Zoco

A fascinating jewellery market in the heart of the Jewish quarter,
with several shops, most of which specialize in the distinctive
filigree silverware.

✉ Avenida de Gran Capitán, Córdoba ☎ No phone

FASHION

Modas Pilar Morales

A chic dress shop between Plaza de las Tendillas and the Avenida
del Gran Capitán.

✉ Conde de Gondomar 2, Córdoba ☎ 957 47 12 54

FOOD AND DRINK

Monsieur Bourguigon

A technicolour array of natural fruit sweets, handmade by Miriam García, awaits shoppers here. Also, fudge and nougat.

✉ c/ Jesús y María 11, Córdoba ☎ 656 33 02 80

SCA Nuestra Señora de la Encarnación

Buy some of Spain's best olive oil – Denominación de Origin Sierra de Cazorla – direct from the producers at their warehouse on the road between Cazorla and Úbeda at the Quesada roundabout. Prices are much lower than in shops and from Dec–Feb you can watch the olives from the surrounding fields being processed.

✉ Carretera A315, Km 22, Peal de Becerro ☎ 953 73 01 09; www.scaencarnacion.es ◷ Mon–Fri 9–2, 4–7; Sat 10:30–1

ENTERTAINMENT

NIGHTLIFE

Café de la Luna

Late-night venue north of La Judería with regular live bands and a varied music policy.

✉ c/ Alhaken II, 12, Córdoba ☎ No phone; www.elcafedelaluna.com ◷ Daily 9pm–3am

La Estrella

Plaza Corredera, east of La Judería and southeast of Plaza de las Tendillas, is a large square enclosed by bars and clubs – La Estrella is just one of many venues, all of which stay open late.

✉ Plaza de la Corredera 14, Córdoba ☎ 957 47 42 60 ◷ Daily 11am–2am

Gongora Gran Café

This large multi-purpose venue, close to Plaza de las Tendillas, is open until the early hours and has a disco, bar and live music.

✉ c/ Gongora, Córdoba ◷ Mon–Sun noon–6 or 7am

La Toscana

Club with large outside terrace for dancing.

✉ Carretera de Trassierra, Km 3, Córdoba

FLAMENCO
Peña Flamenco
Occasional flamenco performances are staged here. Details from the tourist information office.

✉ Conde Romanones 6, Baeza

Tablao Cardenal
One of the best venues for 'classical' flamenco. Performances are staged in a delightful patio, right opposite the Mezquita. Bar and restaurant service. Reservations advised.

✉ c/ Torrijos 10, Córdoba ☎ 957 48 33 20; www.tablaocardenal.com

CLASSICAL MUSIC
Gran Teatro
Córdoba's grand theatre has opera performances, classical concerts (sometimes by the city's own orchestra) and ballet.

✉ Avenida del Gran Capitán ☎ 957 48 02 37; www.teatrocordoba.com

SPORTS AND ACTIVITIES

Extreme Nature Cazorla
Tour operator in Cazorla offering climbing, hiking, canoeing and other activities in the Sierra de Cazorla.

✉ Martinez Falero 52, Cazorla ☎ 649 39 38 31; www.cazorlaextremenature.com

Sierra Cazorla
Activities available in the Sierra Cazorla Parque Natural include trekking, camping, mountain biking, canoeing and horse-riding.

Agencia de Medio Ambiente (AMA)

✉ Tejares Altos, Cazorla ☎ 953 71 15 34

Centro de Interpretación Torre del Vinagre

✉ 16km (10 miles) northeast of Emplame de Valle ☎ 953 71 30 17

TurisNat
The park services in the Parque Natural de Cazorla, Segura y Las Villas operate a range of activities, including four-wheel drive tours of the park and wildlife watching.

✉ Paseo del Cristo 17, Cazorla ☎ 953 72 13 51; www.turisnat.org

Granada and Almería Provinces

Granada

Almería

The provinces of Granada and Almería contain Andalucía's most diverse landscapes. Granada province has the great mountain range of the Sierra Nevada at its heart, where the snow-streaked summit of Mulhacén rises above the foothills of Las Alpujarras. Further east into Almería province, the green dwindles into an increasingly parched landscape of brown and ochre hills.

Both provinces border the Mediterranean, where the holiday areas of the Costa de Almería and the Costa Tropical add to the variety. The city of Granada is famous for its spectacular Moorish Alhambra, one of the world's great architectural treasures, and Almería city boasts its own fortified Moorish palace, the Alcázaba.

The fascinating diversity of the two provinces extends to the towns and villages of the coast and interior, from the beach resort of Mójacar to the mountain villages of Trevélez and Capileira, and from the pottery villages of Níjar and Sorbas to the cave dwellings of Guadix.

GRANADA

Granada stands at the foot of the Sierra Nevada massif, which acts as its dramatic backdrop. Dominating the town is the Alhambra (► 36–37), perched on its hilltop site facing the high ground of the Moorish quarter of Albaicín across the valley of the Río Darro. The Alhambra apart, there is much to see in Granada, from the stately cathedral to the remarkable buildings of the university quarter, and from the fashionable streets of the modern city to the bazaar-like alleyways linking the old city's delightful plazas.

Granada was the last stronghold of the Moors, the final jewel in the crown of the 15th-century Catholic Reconquest of Andalucía. From the early 8th century, the city was controlled from Moorish Córdoba, and then from Seville. In the 1240s Granada emerged as the capital of a separate and successful kingdom under the rule of an independent Arab prince of the Nasrid dynasty. Moorish Granada and its province survived intact for another two centuries until its final conquest in 1492 by Ferdinand and Isabella. Jealous of Moorish grandeur, they set a northern Spanish stamp on Granada, yet preserved the mighty Alhambra, the most spectacular of Andalucía's surviving Moorish monuments.
www.turgranada.es

✚ 20K 🛈 Plaza de Mariana Pineda 10–2 ☎ 958 24 71 28
🕔 Mon–Fri 9–8, Sat 10–7, Sun 10–3

The Albaicín

Granada's antidote to its modern city streets is the engaging Albaicín, the old Moorish quarter that occupies the northern side of the valley of the Río Darro and the hill of Sacromonte, the city's much vaunted *gitano*, or gypsy, quarter. The Albaicín is best reached from Plaza Nueva by following the Carrera del Darro, past the Baños Árabes (► 104) and the Museo Arqueológico (► 107) and on beyond the attractive terrace of

Paseo de los Tristes, where there are numerous cafés in the shade of the Alhambra Hill. You can plunge into the heart of the Albaicín by going along the Carrera del Darro and its continuation of Paseo del Padre Manjón, and then by turning left up Cuesta del Chapiz. Part of the way up, the Camino del Sacromonte leads off right into the gypsy quarter and the notorious 'flamenco caves', where you risk off-loading large sums of money to watch insistent but not entirely authentic flamenco shows.

The real pleasures of the Albaicín lie in the maze of streets and marvellous local plazas, with their bars and restaurants. Find your way to the famous Mirador de San Nicolás for a world-famous sunset view of the Alhambra; but hang on to your bag, *very tightly*; the local thieves are absolute masters at spiriting away anything moveable the minute it is put down.

✚ *Granada 3b*

✉ Northeast of Plaza Nueva

🍴 Numerous bars and restaurants (€–€€) 🚌 Alhambrabus

Baños Árabes

On the way along the Carrera del Darro from Plaza Nueva are the Baños Árabes (Arab Baths), a small but enchanting Moorish bathhouse, entered through a tiny courtyard garden with an inlaid floor and tiny central pool. The 11th-century baths are well-preserved and have the typical star-shape and octagon-shape skylights in the roofs of their brick-vaulted chambers.

✠ *Granada 3b* ✉ Carrera del Darro 31 ☎ 958 02 78 00 ⊘ Tue–Sat 10–2 ✋ Free 🍴 Several in Paseo de los Tristes (€–€€) 🚌 Alhambrabus

Capilla Real

The Capilla Real (Royal Chapel) was built between 1506 and 1521 as a sepulchre for Los Reyes Católicos, Ferdinand and Isabella, one of the most terrifying double acts in history. The Royal Chapel is an

intriguing Gothic building, an odd mixture of the flamboyant and the constrained. It is impressive, yet lacks entirely the subtle elegance of Moorish buildings. Inside lies the Renaissance monument in Carrera marble celebrating the two monarchs. Note how the head of Isabella's effigy is more deeply sunk into her pillow than Ferdinand's – a reflection, it is said, of her undoubtedly superior intelligence. Below the monument, down narrow steps, lie the lead coffins of the monarchs, their daughter Joana and her husband Felipe, although there is no certainty that they contain the genuine remains of anyone.

The most striking feature of the chapel is the altar's superb *retablo* (alterpiece), a gilded extravaganza. In the sacristy are displayed, among royal heirlooms, Isabel's splendid collection of paintings by Flemish masters and others.

➕ *Granada 2c* ✉ Oficios 3 ☎ 958 22 92 39 🕐 Apr–Oct Mon–Sat 10:30–1, 4–7; Sun 11–1, 4–7; Nov–Mar Mon–Sat 10:30–1, 3:30–6:30; Sun 11–1, 3:30–6:30 ♿ Inexpensive 🍴 Bar-Restaurante Sevilla, c/ Oficios 12 (€€) 🚌 1, 3, 4, 6, 7, 8, 9

Catedral

Granada's cathedral stands near the apex of the busy junction of Gran Vía de Colón and Calle Reyes Católicos. The cathedral is crowded round by other buildings, but its massiveness and its stepped exterior of tiled turrets, gables and buttresses rising to a central dome dominate the cramped surroundings. The building dates from the 16th century and reflects all the contemporary certainties that raised it in place of a demolished mosque. The high central dome, supported on huge pillars, lends lightness to the interior and to the wealth of baroque chapels.

➕ *Granada 2c* ✉ Gran Vía de Colón 5 ☎ 958 22 29 59 🕐 Mon–Sat 10:45–1:30, 4–8, Sun and public hols 4–8 (7 in winter) ♿ Inexpensive 🍴 Vía Colona, Gran Vía de Colón 13 (€€) 🚌 1, 3, 4, 6, 7, 8, 9

Monasterio de la Cartuja

The Monasterio de la Cartuja (Monastery of the Carthusians)
lies some way from the city centre, but it is well worth the
journey. This is the most extravagant of Spain's Carthusian
buildings and dates from the early 16th century. The Cartuja's
monastery and church face each other across an attractive patio,
but it is the church that is the real showstopper – it's a lavish
torrent of baroque sculpture, all swirling marble and jasper and
gilded frescoes.

✚ *Granada 1a (off map)* ✉ c/ Real de Cartuja ☎ 958 16 19 32 🕐 Mon–Sun
10–1, 4–8 💷 Inexpensive 🚌 8 C

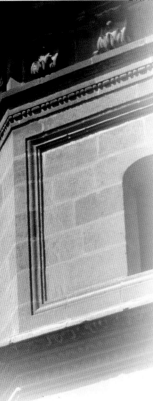

Monasterio de San Jerónimo

The 16th-century Convento de San Jerónimo (Convent of St Jeronimo) lies in the university district to the northwest of the cathedral. The focus of the convent is its central patio, a superb example of mixed Gothic-Renaissance features and with refreshingly peaceful cloisters, where the mellow chanting of the nuns at prayer can often be heard. The adjoining church has an inspiring interior, all painted frescoes and with a glorious four-storeyed *retablo* (altarpiece) within an octagonal apse.

The adjacent university district has a wealth of remarkable churches and secular buildings to offset the lively bustle of student life.

✠ *Granada 1b (off map)* ✉ Rector López Argueta 9 ☎ 958 27 93 37 🕐 Mon–Sun 10–2:30, 4–7:30 ✋ Inexpensive 🍴 Numerous cafés in adjoining San Juan De Dios (€) 🚍 5

Museo Arqueológico

The Museo Arqueológico (Archaeological Museum) is located within a delightful Renaissance palace – the Casa de Castril. The building has a central patio from whose upper balcony you can see the Alhambra across a frieze of tiled roofs. A wide range of exhibits covers the prehistoric, Phoenician, Roman, Visigothic and Moorish periods and is made even by the elegant surroundings.

www.junta-andalucia.es/cultura

✠ *Granada 3b* ✉ Carrera del Darro 43 ☎ 958 22 56 40 🕐 Tue 3–8, Wed–Sat 9–8, Sun 9–2:30. Closed Mon ✋ Inexpensive; free with EU passport 🚍 Alhambrabus, 31, 32

a walk in Granada's Albaicín

From Plaza Nueva walk through Plaza Santa Ana past the Iglesia de Santa Ana y San Gil, and along the narrow Carrera del Darro, keeping a lookout for traffic.

You pass the old Moorish bridge, the Puente de Cabrera, and then the Puente de Espinosa. From here you can see the walls of the Alhambra looming high above.

Continue along Carrera del Darro, passing the Convento de Santa Catalina de Zafra and the Museo Arqueológico on your left. Keep on past the terrace of Paseo del Padre Manjón. After Café Bar La Fuente, turn left up narrow, pebbled Calle Horno del Oro. Go up steps at the top of the alley, then turn right up some more steps. Cross a lane and continue up pebbled Calle Valenzuela. At its top go up more steps, bear left, then turn right at a junction. In 20m (22 yards) go sharply left, then uphill and round to the right. At a junction with Carril de San Agustín, go sharply left and up the pebbled lane. Follow the lane round to the right and keep on, past a junction on the left.

You'll pass the Aljibe de Bibalbonud, a brick-built Moorish well, and Convento Santo Tomasas de Villanueva.

Continue through the tree-lined Placeta del Abad and go alongside the wall of the church of San Salvador. Turn left to reach the entrance to the church.

The church was built on the site of a 13th-century mosque, and the original patio still survives.

Turn left, and then left again into Calle Panaderos. Pass another old well, the Aljibe de Polo, and continue past small shops and bars to reach tree-shaded Plaza Larga. Cross the plaza to its opposite corner and go under the Puerta de la Pesas (Gate of the Weights), a gateway in the old walls of the Albaicín's original Moorish castle. Beyond the arch, climb steps into Placeta de las Minas, turn left along Callejón San Cecilio and follow the lane round right to reach Plaza del Cementerio de San Nicolás.

To the right of the 16th-century church is a Moorish cistern, still spouting water. Immediately in front of the church is the Mirador de San Nicolás, Granada's most famous viewpoint. Keep a strong grip on your belongings here.

Go down the right-hand side of the Mirador, keep downhill, then go right along Nuevo de San Nicolás. At a crossing, turn left onto narrow Cuesta María de la Miel, then at a T-junction turn right along Algibe del Gato. In a few metres, go down left and then round right and into Placeta Nevot. Keep going downhill and on through Placeta de la Cruz Verde. Continue down San Gregorio, then along Calderería Nueva passing Granada's fast-growing modern "Arab quarter". Reach a T-junction with Calle de Elvira, and turn left to return to Plaza Nueva.

Distance 3km (2 miles)
Time 2–3 hours
Start/end point Plaza Nueva ✚ Granada 3b

More to see in Granada and Almería Provinces

ALHAMA DE GRANADA

Alhama, on the lip of a rocky gorge, was a significant Moorish settlement due to its hot springs, *al hamma*. These still attract devotees to the nearby hotel Balneario (➤ 120). The town's main square, the Plaza de la Constitución, is a pleasant place in which to enjoy good tapas at surrounding bars. The Moorish castle at the end of the lower square is privately owned. Nearby is the Iglesia del Carmen, a handsome late-medieval church with a lovely stone fountain outside. On the far side of the Iglesia del Carmen is a terrace overlooking the gorge of the Río Alhama. From the fountain in front of the church, walk with the gorge on your right, to Calle Portillo Naveros, then go left up Calle Baja Iglesia. Pass the charming Casa de la Inquisición, a small building with a perfect façade in the late Gothic/early Renaissance Plateresque style. Then reach the pleasing little square Plaza los Presos and the handsome 16th-century Renaissance church of La Encarnación.

✚ 19K ✉ 40km (26 miles) southwest of Granada 🍴 Café-Bar Andaluz, Plaza de la Constitución (€) 🚌 Mon–Fri Granada–Alhama de Granada

ℹ c/ Vendederas ☎ 958 36 06 86

ALMERÍA

Almería was one of the great cities of Moorish Andalucía, rivalling Seville, but after the Reconquest, the Spanish rulers neglected the port, and a series of earthquakes during the 16th century ruined large parts of the city. Today, Almería has great appeal as an essentially Spanish city with a distinctive North African flavour. Its most enduring monument is the Moorish Alcazaba.

Modern Almería is divided into east and west by the Rambla de Belén, a wide boulevard that has replaced an unsightly dry river bed. West of the Rambla is the Paseo de Almería. Halfway down the Paseo, a broad alley leads to Almería's colourful morning market. At the north end of Paseo de Almería is Puerta de

Purchena, the city's real focus, a busy junction groaning with traffic, but also bustling with life. Calle de las Tiendas, running south from Puerta de Purchena, is one of Almería's oldest streets, now a fashionable shopping venue. Charming side streets lead via Plaza Flores and Torres Siloy to the Plaza San Pedro, with its handsome church and raised promenade.

Just west of Plaza San Pedro is the Plaza Vieja (Old Square), also known as the Plaza de la Constitución. This 17th-century arcaded square, a northern Spanish interloper to Moorish Almería, is entered through narrow alleyways. The central space is occupied by palm trees and a bone-white monument. On the west side is the theatrical façade of the Ayuntamiento (Town Hall).

www.andalucia.org

✚ 22L 🛈 Parque San Nicolás Salmerón ☎ 950 27 43 55

La Alcazaba de Almería

La Alcazaba dominates Almería, although the modern town seems oddly detached from it. The happily scruffy Barrio de Chanca, a district of brightly painted, flat-roofed houses, surges up to its walls. An entrance ramp winds steeply up to Puerta de la Justicia (the Justice Gate), unmistakably Moorish in style. Beyond is the First Precinct, cleverly renovated and reflecting, in its gardens and water channels, what the original must have been like. The views

over the city are superb. A gentle climb past flowering shrubs and tinkling water leads to a beautiful oasis of trees hard against the walls of the Second Precinct. Here marble slabs, inscribed with verses by García Lorca and Fernando Villalón, rest against the wall. Inside the Second Precinct are the foundations of Moorish bathhouses. The Third Precinct encloses the triangular fortress, originally Moorish but greatly strengthened by the Christians. The views are breathtaking. Across the broad valley of San Cristóbal to the west is the Mirador de San Cristóbal, linked to the Alcazaba by the Muralla de San Cristóbal, a distinctive fortified wall.

✉ Almanzor s/n ☎ 950 17 55 00 🕐 Nov–Apr daily 9–6:30; Apr–Nov 9–8:30 💷 Inexpensive; free with EU passport 🍴 Bar/café (€€)

Catedral

Almería's cathedral seems more fortress than church. Its stark and formidable walls were built to repel the pirates and disaffected *Moriscos* who haunted the coast in the aftermath of the Christian Reconquest. Look for the cheerful yet unexplained sun symbol on the east wall, at the entrance to the charming little Plaza Bendicho. The interior is fiercely Gothic and dark, but the choir has outstanding carved walnut stalls and there is a handsome 18th-century altar behind it. A door in the south wall leads to a sunny little Renaissance courtyard, brimming with shrubs and flowers.

✉ Plaza de la Catedral 🕐 Mon–Fri 10–5, Sat 10–1 💷 Inexpensive 🍴 Bodega Montenegro, Plaza Granero (€€) 🚌 Parque de Nicolás Salmerón

LAS ALPUJARRAS

Best places to see, ➤ 38–39.

COSTA TROPICAL

The Costa Tropical is the westward
extension of the Costa de Almería, and
occupies Granada province's Mediterranean
shoreline. It is less developed than its
neighbour and has some spectacular rocky
coastline, a number of pleasant beaches and
attractive resorts such as Almuñécar and
Salobreña. Almuñécar has fine Phoenician,
Roman and Moorish monuments. The
resort's beaches are pebbly and cramped,
but the stylish esplanade of Paseo Puerta
del Mar makes up for this.

🟥 19L ✉ Adra to Almuñécar 🚌 Regular service
Almería–Málaga

GUADIX

Guadix is noted for its splendid cathedral
and for its remarkable cave dwellings. The
former dominates the heart of the town, its
red sandstone walls hiding a darkly Gothic
interior enlivened by baroque forms.
Opposite the cathedral's main doorway is an
archway leading to the Renaissance square
of Plaza de la Constitución, known also as
Plaza Mayor. From the square's far right-
hand corner go up steps and along Calle
Sant Isteban to reach a cluster of handsome
buildings including the Renaissance Palacio
de Peñaflor and its neighbouring 16th-
century church of San Agustín. Between the

two there is a seminary, through which
you gain entrance to the rather down-at-
heel Moorish Alcazaba. To the left of the
Palacio de Peñaflor, in a sunken square, is
the church of Santiago, with a fine
Plateresque door frame.

Walk north from the Alcazaba to reach
the Barrio Santiago, Guadix's famous cave district, where
remarkable dwellings have been carved out of the soft tufa of
tall pinnacles. Visit the **Cueva Museo** for an insight into the
cave culture.

✚ 21K ✉ 60km (37 miles) east of Granada 🚌 Regular services
Granada–Guadix ❓ *Fiestas Patronales de la Virgen de la Piedad*, 6–15
Sep ℹ Avenida Mariana Pineda ☎ 958 69 95 74

Cueva Museo (Cave Museum)

✉ Plaza del Padre Poveda 🕐 Mon–Fri 10–2, 4–6; Sat 10–2
✋ Inexpensive 🍴 Drinks kiosk (€) 🚎 Road train from town centre

MOJÁCAR

There are two Mojácars, and both are busy places. The old
hilltop town of Mojácar Pueblo is hugely popular with the
large number of visitors to Mojácar Playa, the straggling
beach-side development that dominates the coast for several
kilometres. Old Mojácar can still charm in spite of the
summer crowds. Fight your way out of the central Plaza
Nueva and its airy viewpoint of Mirador de la Plaza Nueva,
and climb left to the little garden of Plaza del Sol, then on up
to Plaza del Castillo for more exhilarating views. Head west
from here to explore the narrow flower-bedecked streets and
squares, with their excess of souvenir shops. After all this,
the long narrow beaches of Mojácar Playa are easily reached.

✚ 24L ✉ 65km (40 miles) northeast of Almería 🚌 Almería–Mojácar
❓ Moors and Christians Fiesta, 10 Jun; *Fiestas Patronales San
Augustín*, 25–30 Aug ℹ Plaza Nueva ☎ 950 61 50 25

a drive around the Hills of Las Alpujarras

Take exit 164 off the Motril-Granada highway (A44), signed La Alpujarra. Follow the road uphill until you are higher than the wind turbines on the hillsides. Lanjarón is the first town, the gateway to the Alpujarras. Follow the road through the town. At the first roundabout take the right exit for Órjiva to continue on the A348, then straight over the next roundabout as you leave Lanjarón. Continue on the A348 towards Órjiva. Before you enter the town turn left onto the A4132 to Trevélez. A petrol station stands just before the turning.

Continue to Pampaneira, ignoring all turn-offs. The landscape gets greener and more wooded up here. Before you reach Pampaneira you'll cross the Río Poqueira gorge. Pass through Pampaneira and take the next left signposted for Bubión.

Whitewashed Bubión, overlooking the gorge, is one of the most popular Alpujarran villages.

Beyond the next village, Campileira, the road peters out at the foot of Mulhacén.

Mulhacén is Spain's highest mountain at 3,480m (11,420ft).

Return downhill to the junction with the A4132 through the mountain towns of Pitres, Pórtugos and Busquístar, following signs to Trevélez and Ugíjar.

Beside the road, shops sell cured hams. You're entering the high Sierra Nevada and a view of Mulhacén's snow-streaked peak will fill your windscreen.

At Trevélez, the highest village in Spain, stay on the A4132 – the road veers right. At the top, follow the road to the left for Juviles, which becomes the A4130. At Juviles bear right and head downhill to the foot of the hill. Turn right, signposted Órjiva. At the next junction turn right again for Órjiva, rejoining the A348, which offers stunning views of Las Alpujarras.

The next village is Cádiar; keep left to stay on the A348 to Órjiva. At Órjiva, stay left, following signs for Lanjarón. At Lanjarón, turn left for the A44 Granada-Motil highway.

Distance: Approx 100km (62 miles)
Time: 4 hours (not including stops)
Start/end: Exit 164 off the Granada-Motril road (A44) ✚ 20L
Lunch: La Artesa Restaurante, Bubión (➤ 124)

MONTEFRÍO

This delightful village at the heart of olive-growing country is dominated by the Iglesia de la Villa, a splendid church on a craggy promontory. The other great building is the central Iglesia de la Encarnacíon, a circular neo-classical church, with a domed roof. Montefrío is famous for its sausages, and there are several good restaurants in which to sample them. There are also excellent local varieties of olives and olive oil. To the east, along the road to Illora, is the Neolithic burial site of Las Peñas de los Gitanos.

✚ 19J ✉ 35km (22 miles) northwest of Granada

🍴 Café Bar La Fonda, c/ Amat 7 (€)

🚌 Regular service Granada–Montefrío ❓ *Feria de Verano*, 7–8 Jul; *Fiestas Patronales*, 14–17 Aug

NÍJAR

Ceramics and *jarapas*, light carpets and cloth goods, are specialities of this pleasant village at the foot of the Sierra Alhamilla. There are excellent pottery shops on Avenida García Lorca, the broad main street, and in Barrio Típico Alfarero, leading off from the far end of García Lorca. As always in Andalucían villages, however, you need to go a little further to find the very special places. Walk on from the top of García Lorca past the

tourist office and then up Calle Carretera to the church of Santa María de la Anunciación, which has an excellent *artesonado* coffered ceiling (a panelled timber style of Moorish origin). Keep on to the left of the church, cross Plaza de Granero and continue up Calle Colón, past the covered market, to reach the wonderful Plaza del Mercado, with its overarching elm trees and striking Fuente de la Villa de Níjar, the blue-tiled public fountain with gaping fish-head faucets. Finally leave the top right-hand corner of the square to find, at Lavadero 2, La Tienda de los Milagros (the 'Shop of Miracles', ➤ 128), selling some of the finest ceramic work you could hope to find.

🚹 23L 🖂 30km (19 miles) northeast of Almería 🍴 Café Bar La Glorieta (€€)
🚌 Regular service Almería–Níjar

SORBAS

Sorbas is the village of the *casas colgadas*, the 'hanging houses', a picturesque term that sums up its dramatic clifftop location above a dry valley. There is a strong tradition of pottery-making: the main workshops are in the Barrio Alfarero, in the lower part of the village. The central square, the Plaza de la Constitución, is flanked by the church of Santa María and the old mansions of the dukes of Alba and Valoig. The plaza's central fountain sports the heads of fierce beasts, their mouths crammed with water faucets. As you wander through Sorbas, you will emerge at various *mirador* viewpoints above the cliffs. The village lies at the heart of the Parque Natural de Karst en Yesos, a dramatic limestone landscape.

🚹 24L 🖂 40km (25 miles) northeast of Almería 🚌 Regular service Almería–Sorbas ❓ *Fiesta Cruz de Mayo*, 1–3 May. *Fiesta San Roque*, 14–17 Aug. Guided tours of nearby Cuevas de Sorbas (Sorbas Caves) are available
🛈 Santa Terraplén 9 ☎ 950 36 44 76

Cuevas de Sorbas
☎ 950 36 47 04 ✋ Expensive

HOTELS

ALHAMA DE GRANADA
Balneario de Alhama de Granada (€€)
A long-established spa hotel built over preserved Moorish baths. The hotel has a plain appearance, compensated by its riverside location. Thermal baths and other health treatments are available.

✉ Carretera del Balneario s/n ☎ 958 35 00 11/03 66; www.balnearioalhamadegranada.com

ALMERÍA
Gran Hotel Almería (€€€)
A luxury hotel located at the seaward end of the Rambla de Belén. Close to the old town but out of Puerta de Purchena focus, although it makes up for it with its own disco and swimming pool.

✉ Avenida Reina Regente 8 ☎ 950 23 80 11; www.granhotelalmeria.com

Hotel la Perla (€€)
Said to be the oldest hotel in Almería; family-run. Located just off the Puerta Purchena's busy square, the liveliest part of town, but detached enough from too much street noise.

✉ Plaza del Carmen 7 ☎ 950 23 88 77; www.githoteles.com

Hotel Torreluz III/Hotel Torreluz II (€€–€€€)
Two hotels in an attractive square, and under the same management. Both are associated with excellent restaurants. (There is a third Torreluz hotel in the square. This is AM Torreluz; independent of and more expensive than its namesakes.)

✉ Plaza Flores 3 (Torreluz III); Plaza Flores 6 (Torreluz II) ☎ 950 23 43 99; www.torreluz.com (both hotels)

BÉRCHULES
La Posada (€)
Excellent base for exploring Las Alpujarras. Authentic Alpujarras-style house, hundreds of years old, at the heart of Bérchules. Evening meal and breakfast. Local house wine recommended. English spoken by friendly proprietors.

✉ Plaza del Ayuntamiento s/n ☎ 958 85 25 41

BUBIÓN
Villa Turística del Bubión (€€)
Purpose-built hotel of 43 houses designed as replicas of traditional Alpujarran dwellings, all with terrace or private garden.

✉ Barrio Alto s/n ☎ 958 76 39 09; www.villabubion.com

GRANADA
Alhambra Palace (€€€)
Granada has no shortage of high-end hotels, but this is the most famous of the lot. The palace, with 115 individually decorated rooms, is a marvellous place to stay for even just one night and is just a five-minute walk from the Alhambra itself.

✉ Pena Partida 2 ☎ 958 22 14 68; www.h-alhambrapalace.es

Hostal Camino Real (€)
This easy-to-find *hostal* is on the road up to the Alhambra – it's convenient if you want to get to the Alhambra for the 8am opening time but it's a half-hour walk (or short taxi ride) into the city centre. Rooms are very clean, modern and good value.

✉ Avenida Santa María de la Alhambra, Portal 2, 1a ☎ 958 21 00 57; www.hostalcaminoreal.com

Hotel Carmen (€€€)
Luxurious hotel in the centre of Granada, with all facilities. Special suites, including nuptial suite. Pool terrace with great views. Jewellery and fashion shops for those with the money to spare.

✉ Acera del Darro 62 ☎ 958 25 83 00; www.hotelcarmen.com

Hotel Macía Plaza (€€)
On Plaza Nueva. Excellent location for visiting Granada's major attractions. Some rooms have a good view over this lively square.

✉ Plaza Nueva ☎ 958 22 75 36; www.maciahoteles.com

Hotel Los Tilos (€€)
A traditional no-frills hotel overlooking a bustling plaza with a daily flower market and plenty of café choice.

✉ Plaza Bib-Rambla 4 ☎ 958 26 67 12; www.hotellostilos.com

Parador de Granada (€€€)

Very expensive, top-of-the-range hotel – also top-of-the-hill, with its outstanding location at the heart of the Alhambra. Beautiful surroundings incorporate Moorish features. Reserve ahead.

✉ Real de la Alhambra s/n ☎ 958 22 14 40; www.parador.es

GUADIX
Hotel Comercio (€€)

Prize-winning hotel dating from 1901, beautifully refurbished. Comfortable rooms and lounges, and restaurants serving top local and international cuisine.

✉ c/ Mira de Amezcua 3 ☎ 958 66 05 00; www.hotelcomercio.com

MOJÁCAR
Parador de Mojácar (€€€)

Luxurious hotel complex on Mojácar's sea front. The busy main road passes the gates and you have to cross it to reach the far-from-exclusive beach. However, the hotel has real exclusivity and its facilities include a swimming pool that you need never leave.

✉ Playa de Mojácar ☎ 950 47 82 50; www.parador.es

MONTEFRÍO
Hotel la Enrea (€€)

A very pleasant hotel with modern facilities and excellent service.

✉ Paraje la Enrea s/n ☎ 958 33 66 62

SOLYNIEVE (SIERRA NEVADA)
Melía Sierra Nevada (€€€)

The heated indoor swimming pool has views of the ski slopes. Two restaurants and a bar cater for guests.

✉ Pradallano s/n ☎ 958 48 04 00; www.solmelia.es

TREVÉLEZ
Hotel la Fragua (€€)

Well-placed hotel giving good views of surrounding slopes and with pleasant rooms. The hotel's own restaurant is nearby.

✉ c/ San Antoni 4 ☎ 958 85 86 26; www.hotellafragua.com

VÉLEZ BLANCO
Hostal la Sociedad (€)
Excellent value at this modern, well-appointed *hostal*. Enquire at the emphatically 'local' Bar Sociedad, in the main square, a few metres along the main road.

✉ c/ Corredera 7 ☎ 950 41 50 27

RESTAURANTS

ALHAMA DE GRANADA
Mesón Diego (€)
See page 59.

ALMERÍA
Asador Torreluz (€€)
Part of the Torreluz Hotel complex located on Almería's charming Plaza Flores, this top-class restaurant is renowned for its local and international cuisine.

✉ Plaza Flores 1 ☎ 950 23 49 99 ⊘ Lunch and dinner. Closed Sun

El Bello Rincón (€€)
Considered to be one of Almería's top restaurants, El Bello Rincón offers wonderful sea views as you tuck into the excellent fresh seafood.

✉ Carretera Nacional 340, Km 436 ☎ 950 23 84 27 ⊘ Lunch only. Closed Mon, Jul and Aug

Bodega Las Botas (€€)
This delightful tapas bar is still irresistible. Try to sit at the barrel tables if you're sampling wine – and there's plenty of choice – or at the little tables on the other side of the bar for *jámon* (ham) and fish dishes at their best.

✉ c/ Fructuoso Pérez 3 ⊘ Dinner

BUBIÓN
La Artesa Restaurante (€€)
Attractive split-level small bar and restaurant specializing in roast leg of pork and *choto al ajillo* (kid cooked with garlic). The dark

wood and bright tilework is typically Andalucían. There's parking behind the supermarket opposite.

✉ Carretera de la Sierra 2 ☎ 958 76 34 37 🕔 Lunch and dinner. Closed Sun evenings and Mon

CAPILEIRA
Poqueira (€)
Good little restaurant attached to the hotel of the same name. Local dishes at their best and from a reasonably priced menu.

✉ c/ Doctor Castilla 6 ☎ 958 76 30 48 🕔 Lunch and dinner. Closed Mon

GRANADA
Bodegas Castenada (€€)
Start the evening with tapas and a glass of wine at this grand tapas bar; there's a vast selection. The bar, behind Plaza Nueva, is at the junction of Calle Elvíra, one of the best streets for restaurants in Granada – the others are Calle Navas (for tapas bars) and the plaza Campo del Principe.

✉ c/ Almireceros 1–3, Plaza Nueva ☎ No phone 🕔 Lunch and dinner

Chikito (€€)
Popular 'literary' eating place once patronized by García Lorca and his contemporaries, and by English writers on the romantic Andalucían trail. Just north of the Carrera del Genil promenade in a leafy square. Expensive international dishes, but with a reasonably priced (for Granada) set menu.

✉ Plaza del Campillo 9 ☎ 958 22 33 64 🕔 Lunch and dinner. Closed Wed

Cunini (€)
Popular establishment with a lively atmosphere and a good reputation for its seafood.

✉ Plaza Pescadería 14 ☎ 958 25 07 77 🕔 Lunch and dinner. Closed dinner Sun and Mon

Divisa Blanca Taberna (€€)
At this small, friendly tapas bar the food is cooked behind the bar and you get a small plate of tasty tapas to enjoy with your drink.

The menu is divided into starters and seafood, fish and meat. The décor has a bullfighting theme.

✉ c/ Navas 23 ☎ 958 224 790 🕐 Tue–Sun lunch and dinner. Closed Mon

Mesón El Trillo (€–€€)
Rustic home-cooking is the speciality of this delightful small restaurant in the Albaicín. There's a patio with shaded seating and a cosy interior for the winter months.

✉ Callejón del Aljibe del Trillo, Albaicín ☎ 958 22 51 82
🕐 Lunch and dinner

Mirador de Morayma (€€)
Housed in a handsome 16th-century mansion in the old quarter of Albaicín, this restaurant serves good cuisine. Sit in the delightful leafy terrace, which gives magnificent views over the Alhambra.

✉ Pianista García Carillo 2, Albaicín ☎ 958 22 82 90 🕐 Lunch and dinner. Closed Sun

Restaurante Carmen Verde Luna (€€–€€€)
Trading on its unbeatable views of the Alhambra, this terrace restaurant in the Albaicín, close to the Mirador de San Nicolás, serves modern Andalucían cuisine.

✉ Camino Nuevo de San Nicolás 16 ☎ 958 29 17 94 🕐 Daily lunch and dinner; later in summer

Restaurant Nuevo (€)
The row of tables beside the marble bar at Restaurant Nuevo is always filled with locals or in-the-know visitors. There's a variety of set menus that are exceptionally good value for Granada. Bread, a drink, two courses plus dessert – it won't win awards but it is a bargain.

✉ c/ Navas 25 ☎ 958 22 67 63 🕐 Lunch and dinner

San Nicolás (€€€)
A strikingly elegant restaurant with columns and chandeliers. Choose a table by the window for breathtaking views of the

Alhambra. The menu includes such *nouvelle-Andaluz* dishes as leg of pork filled with lavender and honey.

✉ c/ San Nicolás 3 ☎ 958 80 42 62 🕐 Lunch and dinner. Closed Wed

Sevilla (€€)

This venerable Granadine restaurant located at the heart of the cathedral area offers a reasonably priced menu. There's also a good tapas bar, and a pleasant outside seating area.

✉ Officios 12 ☎ 958 22 12 23 🕐 Lunch and dinner. Closed Sun pm and Mon

Vía Colón (€€)

See page 59.

GUADIX

Comercio (€€)

This top-quality restaurant is located in the hotel of the same name. It has won several prestigious awards for its cooking, so the local and international specialities on offer come highly recommended.

✉ c/ Mira de Amezcua 3 ☎ 958 66 05 00 🕐 Lunch and dinner

MOJÁCAR

Parador de Mojácar (€€€)

You'll find a fine selection of local cuisine in this attractive, modern restaurant, part of the Mojácar *parador* at Playa de Mojácar. Try *gambones de Gaurruchera*, a tasty prawn dish, and don't miss out on the delicious desserts. Reservations are advised for non-residents.

✉ Playa de Mojácar s/n ☎ 950 47 82 50 🕐 Lunch and dinner

TREVÉLEZ

Mesón La Fragua (€)

Located in the hotel of the same name. Good substantial local dishes with *jamón serrano* to the fore.

✉ c/ San Antonio 4 C958 85 85 73 🕐 Lunch and dinner

VELEZ BLANCO

Bar Sociedad (€)

Classic village bar/café where you can sample tapas and *raciónes* in the company of friendly locals and watch the world go by on the small roadside terrace.

✉ c/ Corredera s/n ☎ 950 41 50 27 ⏲ Breakfast, lunch and dinner

Mesón El Molino (€€)

A relaxed eating place tucked away in a narrow alley just off the village's main street. A good range of regional dishes in pleasant and relaxing surroundings.

✉ c/ Curtidores 1 ☎ 950 41 50 70 ⏲ Lunch and dinner. Closed Thu, Sun evening and Jul

SHOPPING

ARTS, CRAFTS, GIFTS AND ANTIQUES

Alfarería Juan Simon

Family-run workshop and shop in the lower town, at the heart of the pottery-making district.

✉ c/ Alfarerías 25, Sorbas ☎ 950 36 40 83

Casa Ferrer

Possibly the best-known music store in the province, dating from 1875; the stock includes elegant hand-crafted guitars.

✉ Cuesta de Gomérez 26, Granada ☎ 958 22 18 32

González Ramos, Taller de Taracea

One of the best of several workshop-galleries producing marquetry (*taracea*).

✉ Cuesta de Gomérez 12, Granada ☎ 958 22 20 70

Gonzálo Reyes Muñoz

A fascinating antiques shop with a strong Spanish element, which should intrigue collectors and casual buyers alike. You'll find enough fine smaller pieces to choose from if you don't have room in your case for some hefty furniture.

✉ c/ Mesones (Placeta de Cauchiles 1), Granada ☎ 958 52 32 74

Juan Fajardo Antiguedades

An antiques shop in the Albaicín; if you're after a bronze of a bull or a kitsch crucifix, Juan will find something.

✉ Carrera del Darro 5, Granada ☎ 696 510 940 (mobile)

Pedro Romero Ruiz

This is one of those Andalucían village shops selling virtually everything. The place to get your genuine sombrero, as worn by local farmers.

✉ General Franco 2, Montefrio ☎ No phone

Ruiz Linares

This is the place to come for a great mix of antiques and *objéts d'art,* including paintings, sculptures, toys and jewellery.

✉ c/ Estribo 6–8 , Granada ☎ 958 22 23 47

La Tienda de los Milagros

This is one of the best places to go if you want to take home some of the distinctive local pottery produced by local workshops in the Barrio Alfarero (Potter's Quarter).

✉ c/ Lavadero 2, Níjar ☎ 950 36 03 59

El Zoco Alpujarreno

Buy one of the ubiquitous Alpujarran rugs at this souvenir shop on a small church square in Pampaneira.

✉ Plaza de la Libertad 10, Pampaneira ☎ 958 76 31 90

BOOKSHOPS
Librería Dauro

A good little bookshop with all types of books.

✉ Zacatín 3, Granada ☎ 958 224521

CHILDREN'S SHOPS
Carrusel

Shoes of all shades and styles for children are on offer in this bright, colourful and friendly little shop.

✉ Tenor Iribarne 11, Almería ☎ No phone

DEPARTMENT STORE
El Corte Inglés
The Granada branch of Spain's do-it-all department store is to the south of the city centre, on a tree-lined boulevard.
✉ Carrera del Genil 20–22, Granada ☎ 958 22 32 40

FASHION
Roberto Verino
Very stylish, cool fashion salon for both men's and women's wear.
✉ Alhóndiga 4, Granada ☎ 958 52 07 48

FOOD AND DRINK
Jamones y Embutidos Chorrillo
If you want to find the best in Alpujarran *jamón*, said to be perfected in the cold air of the mountains, then this Sierra Nevada company has a quarter of a century of experience.
✉ Haza de la Iglesia, Trevélez ☎ 958 85 86 85

Lopez-Mezquita
Mouth-watering and eye-catching displays in this *cafetería-pastelería* offering a huge array of sweet delicacies to tempt even the most jaded palate.
✉ Reyes Católicos 39–41, Granada ☎ 958 22 12 05

ENTERTAINMENT

NIGHTLIFE
El Camborio
Dance club attracting a young crowd, which can get very busy at weekends.
✉ Camino del Sacromonte, Granada ☎ No phone

El Quinto Toro
The Puerta de Purchena is the best area for nightlife in Almería and this tapas bar is one of the best. Close to here, in the Moorish Baths, the Pena El Taranto is the city's best venue for flamenco.
✉ Reyes Católicos 6, Almería ☎ 950 239 135
Pena El Taranto www.eltaranto.net

Music Club Militant Pop

Plays the latest indie bands and hip favourites – with a Britpop slant – in a small, dark room near one of the busiest streets of tapas bars in Granada. Wednesday night is amateur DJ night.

✉ Rosario 10, Granada ☎ No phone; www.fotolog.net/musicclub
🕐 Tue–Sat from 10:30pm

FLAMENCO
Los Tarantos

Touristy but fun flamenco show in the atmospheric setting of the caves of Sacramonte.

✉ Camino del Sacramonte 9, Granada ☎ 958 22 45 25 🕐 Daily from 9pm

SPORTS AND ACTIVITIES

GOLF

East of Malaga, just before Motril, the Baviera golf course is a challenging new course offering views of the Sierra Nevada and the Mediterranean. It's an 18-hole, par-71 course with golf school.

✉ Caleta de Vélez, exit 274 of the E15 coast road ☎ 952 55 50 15;
www.bavieragolf.com

SKIING
Solynieve Ski Resort

Europe's southernmost ski resort is Solynieve, in the Sierra Nevada southeast of Granada. The resort has 86 runs of mainly red and blue levels. It's small, but there's lively nightlife. Peak season is from December to February.

✉ Solynieve ☎ 902 70 80 90; www.cetursa.es

WATER SPORTS
Buceo La Herradura

Diving courses available, from one- to four-day programmes.

✉ Marine del Este, Almuñécar ☎ 958 82 70 83

Puerto Deportivo de San José

Diving in the protected Cabo de Gata Nature Park.

✉ San José, Cabo de Gata ☎ 950 38 00 41

Málaga and Cádiz Provinces

The provinces of Málaga and Cádiz are the most popular of Andalucían destinations – mainly because of Málaga's mass tourism venue, the Costa del Sol, but also because of their spectacular landscapes, old Moorish villages and historic cities and towns. Both provinces have some of the most remote inland and coastal areas in Andalucía. Málaga boasts the remarkable mountain areas of El Torcal and the Sierra Ronda. The Atlantic coast of Cádiz has emptier beaches, and in the north of the province there are spectacular mountain areas, such as the Sierra de Grazalema.

Málaga city has outstanding monuments and a reassuring sense of everyday Andalucían life. Cádiz city has the same authenticity, with the extra magic of its rich history. Fascinating provincial towns, such as Ronda and Jerez de la Frontera, and a host of intriguing villages add to the rich rewards offered by these most southerly provinces.

MÁLAGA

Málaga lies handsomely between the mountains and the sea. It is a busy, friendly city, relatively untouched by the conspicuous tourism of the crowded Costa del Sol, despite being the transit centre for most beach-bound visitors from Northern Europe. The city has lost some of its style through excessive development, but its major monuments, such as the Moorish Alcazaba and its subdued but intriguing cathedral, survive. Many historic buildings have been restored. Beautiful churches, the Museo Picasso, which opened in 2003, and other fine museums, fashionable shops, an excellent mix of bars and restaurants and a persuasive Mediterranean climate all add to Málaga's charm.

Málaga city lies on either side of the Río Guadalmedina, an arid trench for most of the summer. To its west lie large swathes of modern development and what is left of the old district of El Perchel. East of the river, the broad, tree-lined avenue Alameda, the main axis of the city and home to numerous flower stalls, leads to the busy traffic junction of Plaza de la Marina. Beyond it is the delightful Paseo del Parque, a palm-shaded promenade complete with a botanical garden and lined with some fine buildings. Look for the bronze sculpture, *The Jasmine-Seller*, as you stroll in the mellow Málaga evening.

South of the Alameda, a dense block of buildings robs the main city of views to the harbour and to the sea. North of the avenue is the commercial centre, where the area around the market on Calle Atarazanas preserves much of the atmosphere of the old city. East of here are the busy shopping streets that radiate from the lively and diverting Plaza de la Constitución, from which the main street of Calle Larios links the centre with Plaza de la Marina.

Scattered throughout the main centre are numerous bars, cafés and and restaurants, where you can enjoy Malaga's distinctive cuisine, including its famous fried fish. A few steps east from the Plaza de la Constitución take you to the attractive streets and plazas of the historic cathedral district. Above the city is the Alcazaba, on its stepped hill that rises even higher to the Castillo de Gibralfaro.

✚ 18K ✉ 219km from Seville ℹ Pasaje de Chinitas 4 ☎ 952 21 34 45

La Alcazaba

Málaga's Alcazaba has a wonderful sense of antiquity in its rough walls and in the maze of terraces, gardens, patios and cobbled ramps that lead ever upwards through impressive archways into the sunlight. The lower part of the Alcazaba dates from the 8th century, but the main palace is from the 11th century. Málaga's long history is reflected in the partly excavated Roman theatre, below the entrance to the Alcazaba, and in the various marble classical columns embedded within the dark brickwork of the fortress. The upper palace contains the small Museo de la Alcazaba, which displays Moorish artefacts recovered from the site and vicinity, amid decorative patios and rooms. There are magnificent views of Málaga from the ramparts.

✚ *Málaga 4c* ✉ c/ Alcazabilla s/n
☎ 952 12 88 30 🕐 Museo de la Alcazaba Tue–Sun 9:30–8
✋ Inexpensive; Sun free after 2pm
🍴 El Jardín, c/ Canon 1 (€–€€)
🚌 35

Casa Natal de Picasso

You cannot fault a city whose most famous son was one of the world's greatest painters, Pablo Ruiz y Picasso (1881–1973). The Casa Natal Picasso (Picasso's Birthplace) is the headquarters of the Picasso Foundation, and is located in a handsome terrace of 19th-century houses in the large and friendly Plaza de la Merced, with its big central memorial. The building is significant more for its sense of Picasso's presence than for its rather spare (though elegant) rooms, converted out of Picasso's early home. There are some fine mementoes and photographs of the artist, not least the striking photograph in the entrance foyer.

➕ *Málaga 5a* ✉ Plaza de la Merced 15 ☎ 952 06 02 15 ⏰ Daily 9:30–8 ✋ Free 🍴 Several cafés in Plaza de la Merced (€)

Castillo de Gibralfaro

The much-renovated Moorish Castillo de Gibralfaro (Castle of Gibralfaro) stands high above Málaga and above the Alcazaba, to which it is connected by a parapet wall. There are exhilarating views from the

ramparts and from the terraced approach path that leads up from the Alcazaba amid a deluge of bougainvillea and flower beds – but hang on to your wallet or handbag.

➕ *Málaga 6c* ✉ Monte del Faro ☎ 952 22 72 30 ⏰ Daily 9–7:45 ✋ Inexpensive 🍴 Parador de Málaga Gibralfaro (€€€) 🚌 35 from Paseo del Parque. Horse-drawn carriages also make the trip from the Paseo del Parque and from outside the cathedral

Catedral

Málaga's cathedral gets something of a bad press, due perhaps to its lack of a companion for its solitary tower. Another tower was planned originally, but was never constructed – the cathedral is known locally as La Manquita, or the 'one-armed woman'. Building work began in 1528 and was completed in 1783. The cathedral has a strong visual appeal, however, its dark, worn stonework making a pleasing contrast to the more modern buildings that crowd round it. Inside there is much Gothic gloom, in heavily marbled surroundings, with numerous attractive side chapels competing for attention. The *coro*, or choir, is the cathedral's great glory: its fine mahogany and cedar-wood stalls are embellished by carved statues of 40 saints. The adjoining church, the Iglesia del Sagrario, has a Plateresque doorway and a wonderful Renaissance high altar.

✚ *Málaga 3c* ✉ c/ Molina Larios s/n ☎ 952 22 84 91 🕐 Cathedral: Mon–Fri 10–6, Sat 10–5:45. Iglesia del Sagrario: daily 9:30–12:30, 6:30–7:30 ✋ Inexpensive 🍴 El Jardín, c/ Canon 1 (€–€€)

Museo de Artes y Tradiciones Populares

This excellent museum is located in a restored 17th-century inn, the Mesón de la Victoria, built around a little courtyard.

On display is a host of traditional artefacts from the rural and seagoing life of old Málaga province, a rich reminder of a less frenetic age.

✠ *Málaga 2a* ✉ c/ Pasillo de Santa Isabel 10 ☎ 952 21 71 37

⏲ Mon–Fri 10–1:30, 4–7, Sat 10–1:30. Closed Sun and public hols

💶 Inexpensive 🍴 El Corte Inglés Buffet Grill (€), Avenida de Andalucía

Museo Picasso

The long-awaited Picasso Museum finally opened in October 2003. Housed in the handsome 16th-century Palacio de Buenavista, this splendid museum contains a collection of more than 200 Picasso works, including paintings, drawings, sculptures, engravings and some fine ceramics. Some archaeological remains can be viewed in the basement.

✠ *Málaga 4b* ✉ Palacio de Buenavista, c/ San Agustin 8 ☎ 902 44 33 77

⏲ Tue–Thu 10–8, Fri, Sat 10–9 💶 Moderate

More to see in Málaga and Cádiz Provinces

ANTEQUERA

Antequera has great charm behind its busy, unpretentious face. The main street of Infante Don Fernando is full of shops, lively bars and cafés. At its southern end is Plaza de San Sebastián and its church; it is here that old Antequera begins. Beyond the Plaza are the narrow streets of El Coso Viejo, through which the stepped Cuesta de San Judas leads to the Arco de los Gigantes, a 16th-century gateway to the Plaza Santa María and its church. There are exhilarating views from here. Steps lead from the Plaza to the ruined Moorish Alcazaba. On Antequera's northeastern outskirts, on the Granada road, is a group of impressive Neolithic-Bronze Age burial chambers, the Menga and Viera Dolmens.

✚ 17K ✉ 38km (24 miles) north of Málaga
🛈 Plaza San Sebastián 7 ☎ 952 70 25 05

ARCOS DE LA FRONTERA

Arcos de la Frontera is one of Andalucía's liveliest towns. It has outgrown its Moorish hilltop settlement and now spills down from the craggy heights in a long, straggling tail of white buildings above the flat plain of the Río Guadalete. The older, upper part of Arcos is a maze of narrow streets that twist and turn round the churches of Santa María de la Asunción and San Pedro. The former dominates the Plaza del Cabildo, from whose *mirador* there are stunning views of the plain below.

✚ 14J ✉ 50km (31 miles) northeast of Cádiz
🚌 Regular services Cádiz–Arcos, Jerez de La Frontera–Arcos ❓ *Semana Santa* (Holy Week), Mar/Apr; Easter bull-running; *Feria de San Miguel*, end Sep 🛈 Plaza del Cabildo ☎ 956 70 22 64

CÁDIZ

Cádiz captivates without even trying. This is one of the great historic ports of the Mediterranean, with a claim to being the oldest of European cities, and a distinctive peninsular site lending it immense character. The city was founded as *Gaadir* by the mineral-seeking Phoenicians, who exploited the tin and copper of the Sierra Morena. It was also an important port for the Romans and Visigoths. Under later Moorish control the city declined, and even today that distinctive Andalucían Moorishness seems absent from Cádiz. During the 18th century, the decline of Seville as a river port benefited Cádiz and the city became rich on the Spanish-American gold and silver trade.

Today there is a refreshing sense of easy-going life in the maze of streets and squares and along the great sweep of breezy seafront promenades. Tall buildings, salt-eroded and dark-stoned, enclose narrow, shaded alleys that open suddenly into great sun-drenched plazas and gardens and to the glittering Mediterranean. The main square of Plaza San Juan de Dios, with its handsome

Ayuntamiento (Town Hall) and its encircling bars and cafés, makes a lively introduction; and the morning market in Plaza de la Libertad is a blur of colour and movement. The city's splendid churches and museums, its fashionable shops and fine restaurants, its beaches and its flower-decked gardens all combine to make Cádiz a unique experience – even for Andalucía.

www.guiadecadiz.com

www.cadiz.es

✚ 13K ℹ Paseo de Canelejas s/n
☎ 956 24 10 01; Avenida Ramón de
Carranza s/n ☎ 956 25 86 46

Catedral Nueva

The massive New Cathedral is still under restoration but is open to the public – it is wise to check opening times before you visit. The building dates from the prosperous 18th century, and replaced the 'old' cathedral of Santa Cruz. The neo-classical main façade on Plaza de la Catedral is magnificent. It is crowned by a baroque dome, famously 'gilded' yet, in reality, faced with glazed yellow tiles. The interior of the cathedral is a gaunt, stone cavern, classically perfect. Below lies the claustrophobic crypt, which contains the grave of the musician Manuel de Falla.

✉ Plaza de la Catedral ☎ 956 28 61 54 🕓 Tue–Fri 10–1:30, 4:30–6:30, Sat 10–1 💷 Moderate 🍽 Café Bar La Marina, Plaza de las Flores (€€) 🚌 4

Museo de Cádiz

The Cádiz Museum is the pride of Cádiz and one of the best museums in Andalucía. The ground-floor collection is outstanding, especially the Roman displays. On the first floor are paintings by Roger van der Weyden, Murillo, Rubens and Zurbarán, and the top floor has displays of craftwork and a bewitching collection of traditional marionettes.

✉ Plaza de Mina 5 ☎ 956 20 33 68 🕓 Tue 2:30–8, Wed–Sat 9–8, Sun 9:30–2:30 🍴 Cervecería Gaditana, c/ Zorilla (€€) 🚌 2 ✋ Inexpensive; free with EU passport

Oratorio de San Felipe Neri

Of all Cádiz's churches, the Oratorio de San Felipe Neri is the most impressive. In March 1812 the building saw the temporary setting up of the Spanish parliament, or Cortes, that proclaimed the first Spanish Constitution – a radical document whose liberal principles were to influence European politics as a whole. Plaques on the outer wall commemorate leading Cortes deputies. Inside, two tiers of balconies above exuberant chapels complement the high altar and its Murillo painting, *The Immaculate Conception*, all beneath a sky-blue dome.

The nearby Museo Iconográfico e Histórico (Iconographic and Historical Museum) has a marvellous scale model of the late 18th-century city, carved in wood and ivory.

✉ c/ Santa Inés 38 ☎ 956 21 16 12 🕓 Mon–Sat 10–1 ✋ Inexpensive 🍴 Freiduría Las Flores, Plaza de las Flores (€€) 🚌 2

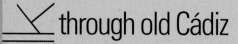

through old Cádiz

A walk through the narrow streets of the old town, seeing a remarkable church on the way.

From the far corner of the Plaza San Juan de Dios, to the right of the Town Hall, go along Calle Pelota and into Plaza de la Catedral. Leave by the far right-hand corner of the Plaza and go along Compaña to the busy Plaza de la Flores. Leave the Plaza to the left of the post office building to reach the market square, La Libertad.

The food market here is in full swing in the mornings.

Leave the market square along Hospital de Mujeres. Turn right along Sagasta and continue to Santa Inés. Go left here and pass the Museo Iconográfico e Histórico to reach the Oratorio de San Felipe Neri (► 141). From the church go down San José, crossing junctions with Benjumeda and Cervantes, then left through Junquería into Plaza de San Antonio.

This vast square is a pleasant place to relax in the sun.

Leave the Plaza on the same side as you entered, but go down Ancha, then go left along San José to Plaza de Mina and the Museo de Bellas Artes y Arqueológico. Take Tinte, to the right of the museum, to Plaza de San Francisco. From the square's opposite corner follow San Francisco through Plaza de San Agustín and on down Calle Nueva to Plaza San Juan de Dios.

Distance 2.5km (1.5 miles)
Time 3 hours, with visits to museums and churches
Start/End point Plaza San Juan de Dios
Lunch El Madrileño (€–€€) ✉ Plaza de Mina

COSTA DEL SOL

Conspicuous tourism is the business of the Costa del Sol, the long ribbon of holiday resorts that runs from Nerja, east of Málaga, along its western shore to Manilva. A sun-seeking break on the Costa has been the aim of millions of tourists over the years and the Costa has responded with gusto.

Resorts such as Marbella and Puerto Banús have an upmarket image and prices to match, while the middle-range resorts of Torremolinos, Fuengirola, Benalmádena Costa and Estepona cover a variety of styles, from 'outgoing' to 'retiring'. All sum up the sea, sun, sand and sangría image. Smaller resorts, such as Sotogrande and San Pedro de Alcántara, now merge with the seamless concrete of the Costa. You will find more Englishness than Andalucían here, but for a good beach holiday, the Costa del Sol is still hard to beat.

🚩 18L ✉ Between Nerja and Gibraltar 🍴 El Portalon, Marbella (➤ 59); many other bars, cafés and resturants along the coast (€€–€€€)

🚌 Regular service from Málaga to all resorts

🚆 Regular service Málaga–Torremolinos–Fuengirola

GIBRALTAR

The wide open spaces of the airport approach to Gibraltar emphasize just how spectacular the famous 'Rock' is. This is the genuine point of contention between Spain and Britain, steeped in nautical history. Gibraltar has been a British colony since 1704 and, although its populace has evolved into an engaging mix of British-Mediterranean character, the buildings, culture, style and especially the commerce are emphatically British. There is enough in Gibraltar to make a visit enjoyable apart from the fascination of the mighty rock: its famous apes, the cable car, St Michael's Cave and views to Africa. Passports must be shown at the police and customs post.

🚩 15M ✉ 120km (75 miles) southwest of Málaga 🚌 Regular services Cádiz–La Linea, Málaga–La Linea, La Linea–Gibraltar

GRAZALEMA

Mountains define Grazalema. They loom like clouds above the village and fill the distant horizon. This is the heart of the Parque Natural Sierra de Grazalema, a spectacular area of harsh limestone peaks softened by vast swathes of the rare Spanish fir, the *Pinsapo*, as well as by cork and holm oak. The *parque* is a superb walking and rock-climbing area, and is reputed to have the highest annual rainfall in Spain.

The impressive peak of San Cristóbal towers above Grazalema. In the charming central square, Plaza de Andalucía, is the attractive church of Nuestra Señora de la Aurora. There is a fountain with amusing faucet heads to the side of a little lane called Agua, which leads to a flower-filled patio ringed by café-restaurants. The craft shop above the tourist office sells locally made produce.

🚌 15K ✉ 20km (12 miles) west of Ronda 🍴 Cádiz El Chico, Plaza de España (€€) 🚍 Regular service Ronda–Grazalema ❓ *Feria de Grazalema*, 22–25 Aug
ℹ Plaza de España ☎ 956 13 22 25

JEREZ DE LA FRONTERA

Best places to
see, ➤ 42–43.

MEDINA SIDONIA

Nothing could be more detached from seagoing than this quiet hilltop town on the edge of the Parque Natural de los Alcornocales, yet Medina Sidonia was the ducal home of the admiral who led the Spanish Armada in its disastrous attack on Britain.

The tree-lined main square, the Plaza de España, is overlooked by the Ayuntamiento (Town Hall). At a shop here, or at the Convento de San Cristóbal in Calle Hercules 1, you can buy some of Medina's famous *dulces* (sweet cakes), such as the almond-flavoured *alfajores*. In the upper town, the church of Santa María la Coronada, in the sunny Plazuela de la Iglesia Mayor, has a very fine altarpiece; behind it are the remains of a Moorish Alcazar. From the Plazuela, a path leads to hilltop views of the surrounding countryside of La Janda.

✚ 14K ✉ 30km (18 miles) east of Cadíz 🍴 Mesón Bar Machín, Plaza Iglesia Mayor 9 (€€) 🚌 Regular service Cadíz–Medina Sidonia

NERJA

These days Nerja is firmly established as part of the Costa del Sol. It is an enjoyable though busy resort with pleasant beaches, and is famed for its Balcón de Europa, a palm-lined promontory on the old belvedere of an original fortress. There is an appealing freshness about Nerja but the form of the old town survives in

its narrow streets. It can be crowded, however, especially at weekends, but it maintains a relaxed air. The cool interior of the simple church of El Salvador, by the Balcón de Europa, reflects this detachment. The best beaches, Calahonda and Burriana, lie to the east of the Balcón. The limestone **Cuevas de Nerja** lie about 4km (2.5 miles) east of the village.

✚ 19L ✉ 52km (32 miles) east of Málaga 🍴 Several cafés and restaurants (€–€€€) 🚌 Regular services Málaga–Nerja, Almería–Nerja ❓ *Carnival*, Feb; *Cruces de Mayo*, 3 May; *Virgen del Carmen*, 16 Jul

ℹ️ Puerta del Mar 4 ☎ 952 52 15 31

Cuevas de Nerja

✉ 4km (2.5 miles) east of Nerja
☎ 952 52 95 20;
www.cuevadenerja.es ☀ Summer daily 10–2, 4–8; winter 10–2, 4–6:30
✋ Moderate 🍴 Restaurant on site (€€) ❓ *Festival de la Cueva* (flamenco and classical music), Jul

RONDA

The dominant feature of picturesque Ronda is the deep gorge (El Tajo) of the Río Guadalevín. Between its towering walls a handsome 18th-century bridge, the Puente Nuevo, hangs like a wedge, groaning beneath the massed weight of visitors. On the south side of the bridge is the old Moorish town. Its focus is the Plaza Duqueza de Parcent, where the fine Iglesia de Santa María Mayor stands on the site of an original mosque. Other places to visit south of the gorge include the Palacio de Mondragón in Calle Manuel Montero, the Minaret de San Sebastian in Calle Armiñan, the Iglesia del Espíritu Santo close to the Puente Nuevo, and the Arab Baths near the Puente Viejo, or Old Bridge, to the east.

On the north side of the Puente Nuevo is the Mercadillo district of modern Ronda. Halfway along Calle Virgen de la Paz is the famous bullring, opened in 1785. It was here that Pedro Romero established the intricate rules of fighting bulls on foot. The attached museum is full of bullfighting memorabilia. From opposite the bullring, stroll up Carrera Espinel, the pedestrianized main shopping street, where you will be spoiled for choice.

🚆 16K ✉ 118km (73 miles) northwest of Málaga 🚂 Málaga–Ronda 🚌 Regular services Málaga–Ronda, Seville–Ronda ❓ *Samana Santa* (Holy Week), Mar/Apr; *Feria y Fiestas de Pedro Romero*, 31 Aug–10 Sep (traditional bullfighting) 🛈 Plaza de España 1 ☎ 952 87 12 72

TARIFA

Tarifa is Europe's most southerly point. Africa is within reach: the blurred outlines of the Moroccan mountains loom across the Strait of Gibraltar, only 14km (9 miles) away. It was at Tarifa that the Moors gained a first foothold on *al-Andalus* in 710. Tarifa is often swept by fierce winds from the stormy bottleneck of the Strait, where the Mediterranean and Atlantic meet head-on. Today, its once remote beaches have been reinvented as world-class venues for windsurfing. You can dodge the wind amid the wriggling lanes and tiny squares and patios of Tarifa's walled Moorish quarter where, in Plaza de San Mateo, the 15th-century Iglesia de San Mateo has a glorious Gothic interior with rich baroque elements. Head west from Tarifa to some of the finest, if often breeziest, beaches around, or visit the impressive Roman ruins at Baelo Claudio, 14km (9 miles) along the coast towards Cádiz (guided visits only).

www.tarifaweb.com

✚ 14M ✉ 90km (56 miles) southeast of Cádiz 🚌 Regular services
Málaga–Tarifa, Cádiz–Tarifa ❓ *Fiesta de la Virgen de la Luz,* 6–13 Sep
ℹ Paseo de la Alameda s/n ☎ 956 68 09 93

VEJER DE LA FRONTERA

The hilltop settlement of Vejer de la Frontera preserves its Moorish character, with an enchanting maze of narrow streets and an old Moorish castle.

✚ 13L ✉ 42km (26 miles) southeast of Cádiz 🚌 Regular service
Cádiz–Vejer. Málaga–Cádiz buses stop on main road below village.
From here, 4km (2.5-mile) steep walk, or taxi

ZAHARA DE LA SIERRA

Best places to see, ➤ 54–55.

a drive through the pine mountains

A drive from Ronda through the spectacular mountain roads of the Parque Natural Sierra de Grazalema.

Leave Ronda, from the north, following signs to Seville and the A374. Stay on the A374 as it drops into the valley, rises again and passes through a gorge. Grazalema and the road through the Sierras, the A372, are signposted left from the A374 – take this turning and stay on the A372 to Grazalema.

The road winds down towards the village past overhanging roadside crags, where you may see rock-climbers.

Continue through Grazalema and in a few kilometres turn off right at a junction (signed Zahara de la Sierra).

This spectacular mountain road through the Sierra Margarita climbs to the Puerta de Palomas Pass, at 1,357m (4,451ft). The mountains are covered in *Pinsapo* pine, a rare species found only in the Grazalema area, cork oak and holm oak. You may see an eagle over the high ground.

Once over the pass, the road follows a series of spectacular hairpin bends that demand concentration, especially since the views are spectacular. At Zahara de la Sierra (▶ 54–55), drive as far as the central square, go round its central point then bear right and follow narrow streets downhill through the one-way system. At the base of Zahara turn left, signposted A339 for Ronda. Follow the road down to the Arroyomolinos recreation area at the edge of the reservoir. Follow the road right, along the edge of the reservoir for Ronda. (Left takes you to Seville and Jerez.) At a junction with the A376, turn right and return to Ronda.

Distance 85km (52 miles)
Time 6 hours, with stops
Start/end point Ronda ✚ 16K
Lunch Los Naranjos ✉ San Juan 15, Zahara de la Sierra ✉ 956 12 33 14; or pick up lunch from the superb delicatessen, Todo Sierra, behind the Plaza de Espana in Grazalema ✉ Plaza Andalucía 23 ☎ 695 55 44 49

HOTELS

ANTEQUERA
Parador de Antequera (€€)

Modern *parador* with all the luxury and good service associated with *paradores*. Surrounded by attractive gardens. Excellent restaurant. Various activities and excursions organized.

✉ Paseo García del Olmo s/n ☎ 952 84 02 61; www.parador.es

ARCOS DE LA FRONTERA
Hotel La Fonda (€)

A delightful hotel in the busy lower town, but within easy reach of the old centre. La Fonda was originally a coaching inn dating from the mid-19th century. Its restaurant is in the converted stables. High ceilings, wooden galleries and hand-made tiling all add to the atmosphere.

✉ c/ Corredera 83 ☎ 956 70 00 57; www.hotelafonda.com

Los Olivos (€€)

Delightful, small hotel right in the heart of the old town. All modern facilities, yet with traditional style reflected in its beautiful patio. Hotel restaurant is recommended for excellent local cuisine.

✉ San Miguel 2, Boliches ☎ 956 70 08 11; www.hotelolivosarcos.com

Parador de Arcos de la Frontera (€€€)

A prime location on the Plaza del Cabildo adds to the cachet of this luxury *parador*. Moorish and Mudéjar décor and furnishings throughout, and fine views from many of the balconied rooms. The restaurant serves traditional local cuisine.

✉ Plaza del Cabildo s/n ☎ 956 70 05 00; www.parador.es

CADÍZ
Hostal Bahia (€)

Excellent-value small pension near the central Plaza de San Juan de Dios. Most rooms have balconies and all are attractively furnished with modern bathrooms. Recommended restaurant, Mesón La Nueva Marina, right next door.

✉ c/ Plocia 5 ☎ 956 25 90 61

Hostal Fantoni (€)

This delightful small *hostal* is tucked away in an otherwise dull side street off Plaza Juan de Dios. Marble staircases and *azulejos* tiles are everywhere. Small but spotless rooms. Hugely popular, so reservations advised.

✉ Flamenco 5 ☎ 956 28 27 04

Parador Hotel Atlántico (€€€)

Overlooking the sea and with direct access to the beach, this classic *parador* has all the luxurious facilities you would expect. There is also a good restaurant offering traditional and international cuisine.

✉ Avenida Duque de Nájera 9 ☎ 956 22 69 05; www.parador.es

ESTEPONA
Atalaya Park Golf Hotel and Resort (€€€)

The Atalaya Park hotel combines the appeal of a luxurious resort with a new and improved golf course in exclusive Estepona. Facilities are extensive, with swimming pools, childcare, bars, restaurants, sports equipment for rent and good access for people with disabilities.

✉ Estepona, Carretera Cádiz-Málaga, Km168 ☎ 952 88 90 00; www.atalaya-park.es

GIBRALTAR
Bristol (€€)

A smart, mid-price hotel, but still near the top end of the range, for quality – like most things in Gibraltar. Good location, near the cathedral, and with its own garden and pool.

✉ 10 Cathedral Square ☎ 350 76800

GRAZALEMA
Villa Turística de Grazalema (€€€)

Near the village of Grazalema, in fine surroundings, this luxury hotel has good facilities enhanced by its own gardens, pool and restaurant.

✉ Carretera Comarcal 344 ☎ 956 13 21 36; www.tugasa.com

JEREZ DE LA FRONTERA

El Ancla Hotel (€)

Delightful small hotel in typical Andalucían building with wrought-iron balconies and yellow paintwork. Rooms are plainly furnished but clean and comfortable; underground parking nearby.

✉ Plaza del Mamelón ☎ 956 32 12 97; www.hotel-ancla.com

MÁLAGA

Hotel Venecia (€)

Central location on Málaga's main avenue, down by the Plaza de la Marina. Basic facilities, spacious rooms. Good value.

✉ Alameda Principal 9 ☎ 952 21 36 36

Larios (€€€)

Smart hotel in the city centre's most fashionable shopping street, near the cathedral. Black-and-white tiles, cool beige furnishings and pine make for a modern, upbeat look. Some of the rooms overlook the lovely Plaza de la Constitución.

✉ Marqués de Larios 2 ☎ 952 22 22 00; www.hotel-larios.com

Málaga-Gibralfaro (€€€)

Splendid *parador* located high above the town on the Gibralfaro hill, with glorious views across the bay.

✉ Castillo de Gibralfaro s/n ☎ 952 22 19 02; www.parador.es

NERJA

Hotel Balcón de Europa (€€)

Located at the heart of Nerja, adjoining the Balcón de Europa and with access to Caletilla Beach.

✉ Paseo Balcón de Europa 1 ☎ 952 52 08 00; www.hotelbalconeuropa.com

RONDA

Hotel Don Miguel (€€)

A comfortable small hotel with pleasant rooms and some spectacular views of Ronda's famous gorge.

✉ c/ Villanueva 4 ☎ 952 87 77 22; www.dmiguel.com

Parador de Ronda (€€€)

Ronda's 18th-century town hall now functions as a lavishly restored and delightful *parador*, with many of its rooms overlooking the deep gorge that has made Ronda famous.

✉ Plaza de España s/n ☎ 952 87 75 00; www.parador.es

TARIFA
Hurricane Hotel (€€)

Wonderful, if windswept, hotel on the beach; a favourite among windsurfers.

✉ Carretera Cádiz-Málaga, Km 77 ☎ 956 68 49 19

ZAHARA DE LA SIERRA
Arco de la Villa (€€)

Small, modern hotel in an enviable position on Zahara's rocky outcrop.To reach it, go all the way through the village and then continue uphill towards the castle.

✉ Camino Nazari s/n ☎ 956 12 32 30

RESTAURANTS

ANTEQUERA
El Angelote (€€)

Centrally located across from the museum, this excellent restaurant serves fine local cuisine. Try the *setas* (oyster mushrooms) with garlic and rosemary, or wild partridge. The desserts are delicious and varied.

✉ c/ Encarnación (corner Coso Viejo) ☎ 952 70 34 65 ◷ Lunch and dinner. Closed Mon

ARCOS DE LA FRONTERA
El Convento (€€)

Pleasant restaurant of the hotel of the same name, at the heart of the old town. Outstanding traditional cuisine, with game dishes a speciality. You pay less for the set menu, but this is still relatively expensive.

✉ c/ Maldonado 2 ☎ 956 70 32 22 ◷ Lunch and dinner. Closed 17–22 Jan

CÁDIZ

Balandro (€)
A local favourite, with a pleasant terrace as well as an inside dining area. Excellent Cádiz fish and seafood tapas, and *raciones*.
✉ Alameda Apodaca 22 ☎ 956 22 09 92 🕐 Lunch and dinner

Cádiz (€)
See page 58.

El Alijibe (€€–€€€)
of traditional recipes with contemporary cooking techniques using ingredients from Cádiz's market. The bar serves great tapas while a dining room offers a grander experience.
✉ c/ Plocia 25 ☎ 956 26 66 56 🕐 Lunch and dinner

El Faro (€€)
Rated as one of the best fish restaurants around. The *paella* is great, as are the local dishes featuring bream, octopus and hake.
✉ c/ San Félix 15 ☎ 956 22 9916 🕐 Lunch and dinner

Mesón Cumbres Mayores (€–€€)
Good lively tapas bar and restaurant. A great variety of dishes include fish, seafood and barbecued meats.
✉ c/ Zorilla ☎ 956 21 32 70 🕐 Lunch and dinner

Pazza Mina (€)
Enjoy delicious artisanal ice cream in one of Cádiz's smaller squares. Pazza Mina's ice creams and sorbets are all handmade.
✉ Plaza de Mina 15 ☎ 956 21 28 80 🕐 Daily from noon

GIBRALTAR

La Bayuca (€€€)
One of the oldest restaurants on the Rock, well known for its Mediterranean specialities, with an extensive menu and emphasis on seafood. Delicious desserts and swift, friendly service.
✉ 21 Turnbull Lane ☎ 956 77 51 19 🕐 Lunch and dinner. Closed Sun lunch and Tue

JEREZ

El Gallo Azul (€)

Central tapas bar with a high turnover and some award-winning tapas, making it a good bet when other bars are closed or crowded. Very inexpensive.

✉ c/ Large 2 ☎ 956 32 61 48; www.casajuancarlos.com 🕔 Daily lunch and dinner until late

Gaitán (€€)

See page 58.

MÁLAGA

Bar Lo Güeno (€)

This is one of the best-known tapas bars in Málaga, with more than 75 varieties to choose from. The L-shaped bar is very cramped, but there are tables outside if you like more space. Excellent range of Rioja wines.

✉ c/ Marín García 9 ☎ No phone 🕔 Lunch and dinner. Closed Sun

Casa Pedro (€–€€)

Long-established, family-run fish restaurant in El Palo. The dining-room overlooks the sea and the seafood is very fresh. If you don't mind the noise and bustle, come here for Sunday lunch, when Malagueño families traditionally dine out

✉ Quitapenas 121, El Palo ☎ 952 29 00 13 🕔 Lunch and dinner. Closed Mon

El Chinitas (€)

See page 58.

Flor de Lis (€)

Flor de Lis is a café serving design-your-own salads and pasta with chill-out music in an old building overlooking the Plaza de la Merced. It's one of the few free wi-fi enabled venues in the city.

✉ Plaza de La Merced 18 ☎ 952 21 44 53; www.flordelis.net
🕔 Lunch and dinner

El Trillo Taberna (€€)

Feast on scrambled eggs, stuffed pepper and other Iberian dishes in this little triangle of restaurants east of Marques de Larios.

✉ c/ Don Juan Díaz, Esquero Larios ☎ 952 60 39 20 🕐 Lunch and dinner

MARBELLA
Santiago (€€€)

Elegant restaurant with a good position on the seafront. Offers top-quality fish and seafood, along with an extensive wine list.

✉ Paseo Marítimo 5 ☎ 952 77 43 39 🕐 Lunch and dinner. Closed Nov

El Portalon (€€€)

See page 59.

MEDINA SIDONIA
Bar Cádiz (€)

Centrally located bar-restaurant with a traditional menu and a good selection of tapas.

✉ Plaza España 14 ☎ 956 41 02 50 🕐 Lunch and dinner

NERJA
Casa Luque (€€)

One of Nerja's best-known establishments, housed in an old Andalucían mansion. Cuisine is from the north of Spain. The attractive patio is open for outdoor dining in summer.

✉ Plaza Cavana 2 ☎ 952 52 10 04 🕐 Lunch and dinner

RONDA
Pedro Romero (€€)

Popular, award-winning restaurant; walls covered in bullfighting photographs. *Rabo de toro a la Rondeña*, Ronda-style bull's-tail stew, is a speciality; or try the grilled salmon.

✉ Virgen de la Paz 18 ☎ 952 87 11 10 🕐 Lunch and dinner

El Molino (€–€€)

See page 59.

Restaurant Don Miguel (€€)

Restaurant in a hotel of the same name, with indoor eating and spacious terraces on several levels offering dramatic views of Ronda's gorge.

✉ c/ Villanueva 4 ☎ 952 87 77 22 🕐 Lunch and dinner

SANLÚCAR DE BARRAMEDA
Casa Bigote (€€)

The standard of fish cuisine is high in Sanlúcar, so restaurants with good reputations are of a very high standard indeed, and El Bigote is one of the best.

✉ Bajo de Guía s/n ☎ 956 36 26 96 🕐 Lunch and dinner

TARIFA
Bar Morilla (€)

Pleasant tapas bar with outside seating, at the very heart of the town. Good selection of local dishes.

✉ c/ Sancho IV El Bravo s/n ☎ 956 68 17 57 🕐 Lunch and dinner

TORREMOLINOS
Bodega Quitapenas (€)

Much favoured by locals and tourists for its reasonably priced tapas and seafood dishes, and its position on the steps leading down to the beach. Always a hive of activity.

✉ c/ Cuesta del Tajo 3 🕐 Lunch and dinner

SHOPPING

FASHION
El Corte Inglés

Málaga's branch of Spain's venerable department store, good for anything from cosmetics to clothing.

✉ Avenida Andalucía 4–6, Málaga ☎ 952 07 65 00

Donna Piu

Exciting fashions from Italian designer collections, to go with the general high-fashion look in this trendy resort.

✉ Benabola, Puerto Banús ☎ 952 81 49 90

FOOD AND DRINK

Bodega González Byass

Jerez is renowned for its sherry and there are dozens of bodegas around the city offering tours, tastings and competitive prices for bottles of *fino*. One of the closest to the city centre is the González Byass bodega south of the cathedral, where the tour includes a trip to a vineyard by train and wine tasting. Other big names offering bodegas tours in Jerez include Harveys and Sandeman.

✉ c/ Manuel María González 12, Jerez de la Frontera ☎ 956 35 70 00; www.bodegastiopepe.com ◷ Tours: Mon–Sun hourly 11:30–5:30

La Mallorquina

One of the city's many wonderful delicatessens, with a mouth-watering window display of great wheels of *Manchego* cheese, cold cuts, nuts, dried fruits and locally produced *turrón* (nougat) and marzipan. This is also the place to pick up your Málaga wine made from sweet muscatel grapes.

✉ Plaza de Félix Sáenz, Málaga ☎ No phone

Todo Sierra

This delicatessen is proudly stocked with products from the Sierra de Grazalema, including preserves, oils, delicious cheeses and hams.

✉ Plaza Andalucía 23, Grazalema ☎ 695 55 44 49

JEWELLERY

Arco

This is one of those tucked-away shops with some appealing jewellery and accessories. It also does a charming line in mobile phones.

✉ c/ San José 23, Cádiz ☎ 956 22 30 71

Joyería Monaco

A wide selection of jewellery, gold and silver work, as well as porcelain and crystalware.

✉ Larga 17, Jerez ☎ 956 33 18 37

Nicholson
Fashionable jewellery products and accessories, including earrings and bracelets.

✉ c/ Marbella s/n, Fuengirola ☎ 952 47 58 82

ENTERTAINMENT

NIGHTLIFE

Casino Marbella
Blackjack, roulette, poker and slot machines.

✉ Bajos del Hotel, Andalucía Plaza, Marbella ☎ 952 81 40 00; www.casinomarbella.com 🕐 Slot machines: 4pm–early hours. Casino: 8pm–early hours; passports must be shown. Restaurant: 9pm–3am

Casino Torrequebrada/Fortuna Night Club
The place to come for blackjack, roulette, poker, slot machines and a glitzy floor show. Passports must be shown at reception.

✉ Avenida del Sol, Benalmádena Costa ☎ 952 44 60 00 🕐 Daily 9pm–4am

Club Naho
Although much of Cádiz's nightlife takes place on the Punta, there are bohemian options in the old town, principally this louche bar-club between Plaza de Mina and Plaza Espana.

✉ Beato Diego de Cádiz 8, Cádiz ☎ No phone; www.nahocadiz.es

El Malecón
One of the most popular spots for Latin-style dancing.

✉ Paseo Pascual Pery, by Punta de San Felipe, Cadíz ☎ 956 22 45 19

Moochers Jazz Café
Live music and giant pancakes are on offer in this popular jazz and Hollywood themed bar-restaurant.

✉ c/ de la Cruz 17, Fuengirola ☎ 952 47 71 54

Oliviere Valeres
Late-night venue decorated in mock Moorish style. Huge dance floor and a variety of bars. Terrace for cooling off.

✉ Carretera Istan, Marbella ☎ 952 82 88 61 🕐 Daily 8pm–4am

O'Neill's Irish Pub
Popular for draught Guinness and big doses of Irish music.
✉ c/ Luis del Velázquez 3, Málaga ☎ 952 60 14 60

Sala Vivero
Hiphop, reggae and indie rock venue in Málaga – an antidote to the cheesy nightclubs in the resorts.
✉ c/ Parauto, Polígono La Estrella, Málaga ☎ No phone;
www.salavivero.com

Tivoli World
There is a full range of musical entertainment here, including flamenco, country and western, and popular musicals.
✉ Arroyo de la Miel, Benalmádena Costa ☎ 952 57 70 16

THEATRE
Gran Teatro Falla
Cádiz's grand theatre has a packed calendar of music, theatre and musicals. Shows range from *Macbeth* to *Grease*.
✉ Plaza de Falla, Cádiz ☎ 956 22 08 34

FLAMENCO
Fundación Andaluza de Flamenco
Authentic 'classical' flamenco at its best.
✉ Plaza San Juan 1, Jerez de la Frontera ☎ 856 81 41 32

Teatro Miguel de Cervantes
Regular flamenco shows are staged at this theatre.
✉ Ramos Marín s/n, Málaga ☎ 952 22 41 00

SPORTS AND ACTIVITIES
HORSE-BACK RIDING
Escuela de Arte Ecuestre 'Costa del Sol'
Riding centre where you learn about the skills required to handle these famous Andalucían horses. Weekly dressage displays.
✉ Carretera Natcional 340, Km 159, Río Padrón Alto s/n, Estepona
☎ 959 44 24 66; www.escuela-ecuestre.com

Hípica International

Half-day rides are available for experienced riders; also jumping and dressage lessons.

✉ Camino de la Sierra, Torremolinos ☎ 695 10 48 48

Real Escuela Andaluza del Arte Ecuestre
(Royal Andalucían School of Equestrian Art)

This is an unmissable experience. Even if horses are not your passion, they will become so during this superb display. Enjoy breathtaking equestrian movements in the Royal School's handsome arena.

✉ Avenida Duque de Abrantes, Jerez ☎ 956 31 80 08; www.realescuela.org
🕐 Mon, Wed, Fri displays at 11 and 12:30; Tue, Thu at noon; Sat open 11–1.
Tours of stables and training sessions available 🖐 Expensive

GOLF

Golfing visitors to Andalucía will find plenty of choice.

Alhaurin Golf & Country Club

45 holes, par 72. Reasonable green fee.

✉ Mijas-Alhaurín el Grande, Málaga ☎ 952 59 59 70

Estepona Golf

18 holes, par 72. Reasonable fee.

✉ Apartado 532, Estepona ☎ 952 11 30 81

Golf Club Marbella

18 holes, par 71. Expensive.

✉ Carretera de Cádiz, Marbella ☎ 952 83 05 00

Golf Torrequebrada

18 holes, par 72. Moderate fee.

✉ Carretera de Cádiz, N340, Benalmádena ☎ 952 44 27 42

La Quinta Golf & Country Club

27 holes, par 72. Moderate fee.

✉ Carretera de Ronda, Km 3.5, Marbella ☎ 952 76 23 90

HANG-GLIDING AND PARAGLIDING

In the Valle de Abdalajís, near Málaga, thermal conditions are especially good for hang-gliding and paragliding.

Club Vuelo Libre Málaga

Week-long beginners' courses available. Also two-seater flights with instructor. Accommodation available.

✉ Valle de Abdalajís s/n ☎ 952 48 92 98

HOT-AIR BALLOONING
Aviación del Sol

Organizes hot-air balloon trips over land and sea.

✉ Apartado 344, Ronda ☎ 952 87 72 49

ADVENTURE SPORTS
Horizon

Horizon offers a whole range of outdoor activities in Sierra de Grazalema's Parque Natural, including caving, rock-climbing, mountain biking, paragliding and trekking.

✉ c/ Agua 5, Grazalema ☎ 956 13 23 63; www.horizonventura.com

WATER SPORTS
Club Nautico Diving Centre

Diving courses available all year at the marina.

✉ Puerta Marina, Benalmádena s/n, Benalmádena Puerta Deportivo
☎ 952 56 07 69; www.benalmadena.com

Tickets-to-Ride

Individual and group canoeing trips.

✉ Istán Lake, Istán (20 minutes from Marbella) ☎ 609 51 75 17

WINDSURFING

The Costa del Luz is noted for its excellent wind-surfing conditions, especially in its southern section.

Club Mistral

✉ Hurricane Hotel, Tarifa ☎ No phone; www.club-mistral.com

Seville and Huelva Provinces

Andalucía's most westerly provinces of Sevilla (Seville) and Huelva are precisely defined by the hills of the Sierra Morena in the northwest and by the fertile plain of the Río Guadalquivir, La Campiña, in the southeast. The Sierra Morena is the least-populated part of Andalucía, and although these hills lack the spectacular ruggedness of other ranges, their tree-covered slopes and scattered villages have an appealing remoteness. The region's coastline is contained mainly within Huelva province and includes the great delta of the Guadalquivir and the Parque Nacional de Doñana.

Seville lies at the heart of the region. This is Andalucía's capital and

its most fashionable city, home to magnificent monuments and with a cultural life to match any city in Europe. Huelva city is a more mundane, workaday place, fuelled by industry, but with some fine churches and museums.

SEVILLE

Seville is one of the most exciting cities in Europe. It is crammed with elegant shops, bars and restaurants, yet within the old quarter of the Barrio Santa Cruz lies a tangle of shaded alleyways, plazas and patios of almost village-like character. The great monuments of the cathedral, the Giralda and the Reales Alcázares apart, Seville has numerous other superb attractions. The vibrant cultural and social world of the city spills over into almost every aspect of life, mixing the very best of the past with modern elegance and fashion.

Seville generates style and romance like heat from the sun. Think Carmen and Don Juan and you have some measure of the city's passionate, if sometimes theatrical, character. Yet there is an easy-going element about Seville that is essentially of the Mediterranean.

The city evolved as a historic trading centre for the gold and silver of the Sierra Morena. It was controlled by the Romans and then by the Moors from 712 until the Christian conquest of 1258. The discovery of the Americas made Seville one of the greatest ports and cities in Europe. Decline came with the silting of the Guadalquivir, but the glory of Seville has lasted into modern times.

Seville's main focus is its magnificent cathedral and Giralda tower (➤ 168–169) and the adjacent Alcázar (➤ 50–51). The cathedral and La Giralda are among the most visited monuments in Europe, but the weight of people does not diminish the fact that these are stunning buildings. South of the cathedral, beyond the Avenida de la Constitución, is the commercial district. Northeast of the cathedral is the delightful old Jewish quarter of Barrio Santa

Cruz (► below), while a little farther north is one of Seville's hidden gems, the 16th-century mansion La Casa de Pilatos (► 168), claimed to be based on Pontius Pilate's house. Southeast of the cathedral are the public spaces of Plaza de España and the María Luisa Park. To the north lie the bustling Plaza de San Francisco and the great canopied shopping street of Calle Sierpes and its neighbours.
www.turismosevilla.org

🏠 5D 🛈 Avenida de la Constitución 21 ☎ 954 22 14 04

Barrio Santa Cruz

A first experience of the tightly knit alleyways of the Barrio Santa Cruz can seem claustrophobic. Tall buildings shut out the sun; their stonework is dark and gloomy; the mood seems more northern European than Andalucían. But the Barrio eventually captivates. Santa Cruz was the *aljama*, or Jewish quarter, of the medieval city and was greatly changed after the Jewish community was expelled in 1492.

The area was much restored and refurbished in the first years of the 20th century, and its narrow, muffled streets are a wonderful antidote to the raging traffic of Seville's busy main thoroughfares. Wander at will or follow a plan (► 64) and soon you will discover flower-filled corners such as Plaza Santa Cruz, the Jardines de Murillo on the Barrio's eastern boundary and the Plaza Doña Elvira. There are numerous bars and cafés in which to take a break along the way.

🏠 *Sevilla 3b* ✉ East of the cathedral
🍴 Bars, cafés and restaurants (€–€€€)

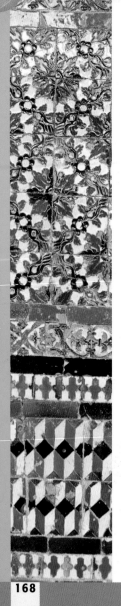

La Casa de Pilatos

Pilate's House is one of Seville's finest treasures. Built in 1519, the house was said to be a copy of Pontius Pilate's house in Jerusalem, but there is no real evidence confirming this. The entire building is a glorious celebration of the Mudéjar style mixed with the most elegant of Italianate features. The *azulejos* tiling is outstanding; the patios, arcades, stairways and richly furnished salons are all superb. This is the best place to truly get a feel for the subtle complexities of this unique architecture. There is hardly a finer self-contained complex of late medieval style and design in all of Andalucía.

✚ *Sevilla 3a* ✉ Plaza Pilatos 1 ☎ 954 22 52 98 🕐 Daily 9–6 (summer 9–7) 💷 Expensive 🍽 Bodega Extraména, c/ San Esteban (€€) 🚌 C1, C2, C3, C4 (for Plaza San Agustín)

La Catedral y La Giralda

Seville's cathedral is said to be the largest Gothic church in the world. It replaced a Muslim mosque, and was a gesture of unashamed Christian triumphalism. The cavernous interior seems almost too vast to express anything other than empty pride, but the magnificent altarpiece in the sanctuary, intense focus of countless guided groups, is breathtaking in its exuberant design. The choir and Renaissance Capilla Real (Royal Chapel) are just as striking. Outstanding works of art and religious artefacts fill the cathedral, and the alleged tomb of Christopher Columbus makes an eye-catching theatrical piece.

You can achieve momentary fitness, or exhaustion, by climbing the Giralda – although at busy times tackling the tower's 34 ramps and 17 final steps becomes something of a weary trudge. The Giralda is the surviving 12th-century minaret of the original mosque, a structure that was heightened in 1565 by the addition of a bell tower and crowned by a bronze weather vane (*giraldillo*). The tower's exterior is its true glory, but the views from its upper gallery are impressive.

www.catedralsevilla.es

✚ *Sevilla 2b* ✉ Plaza Virgen de los Reyes ☎ 954 21 49 71 🕐 Mon–Sat 11–5, Sun 2.30–6 (summer Mon–Sat 9:30–4) 🍴 Numerous restaurants in c/ Mateos Gago (€–€€€) Ⓤ Moderate; free Sun 🚌 Avenida de la Constitución

Itálica

The Roman ruins of the city of Itálica lie 9km (5.5 miles) north of Seville and can be reached by bus from the city's Plaza de Arma bus station.

➕ 5D ✉ Santiponce ☎ 955 99 65 83 🕐 Closed Mon and festivals

Museo del Baile Flamenco

Finally, Seville has a museum dedicated to the dance that touches every facet of the city's character: flamenco. The Museo del Baile Flamenco, which opened in 2006, prides itself on its interactivity; there are frequent workshops in the basement, so even if you have less than metronomic timing, have a go at it. On the upper levels there are costume displays, video shows and photographic exhibitions. What the museum imparts is a passion for flamenco, which, after all, is exactly what the dance is about.

www.museoflamenco.com

➕ *Sevilla 2a* ✉ c/ Manuel Rojas Marcos 3 ☎ 954 34 03 11 🕐 Apr–Oct daily 9–7; Nov–Mar daily 9–6 ✋ Moderate 🚌 Avenida de la Constitución

Museo de Bellas Artes

The Fine Arts Museum, in the beautiful old convent La Merced Calzada, is one of Spain's major art galleries. Highlights are works by Zurbarán and Murillo, including the latter's *Virgin and Child*, the famous 'La Servilleta', so named because the 'canvas' is said to be a dinner napkin.

There are other works by Goya, Velázquez and El Greco. Room 5, once the convent church, is dazzling, with its painted roof and Murillo collection.

✚ *Sevilla 2a* ✉ Plaza del Museo 9 ☎ 954 78 65 00 ⏰ Tue 2:30– 8:30, Wed–Sat 9–8:30, Sun 9–2:30 💰 Inexpensive; free with EU passport 🚌 C3, C4, C5, 6, 43

Plaza de España and María Luisa Park

Semicircular Plaza de España is fronted by a short length of canal, spanned by ornamental bridges. María Luisa Park is a glorious stretch of wooded gardens, drenched in flowering plants. Beyond are the Museo Arqueológico and the Museo de Artes y Costumbres Populares (Popular Arts Museum).

✚ *Sevilla 3c* ✉ Avenida de Isabel la Católica

Reales Alcázares

Best places to see, ➤ 50–51.

More to see in Seville and Huelva Provinces

ARACENA

Aracena's most lauded attraction is the the Gruta de las Maravillas (Grotto of Marvels, ➤ 40–41). But Aracena and its surroundings have much to offer above ground. The town surrounds a hilltop medieval castle ruin and its adjacent church of Nuestra Señora de los Dolores; there are pleasant bars and cafés nearby.

www.aracena.es

✚ 4B ✉ 89km (55 miles) northwest of Seville 🍴 Several (€–€€)

🚌 Regular services Seville–Aracena, Huelva–Aracena

ℹ St Pozo de la Nieve ☎ 959 12 82 06

AROCHE

The charming hilltop village of Aroche lies only 24km (15 miles) from the border with Portugal. Its Moorish castle, established in the 9th century, was rebuilt substantially in 1923 and now incorporates one of Andalucía's most eccentric bullrings, as well as the village's archaeological museum. Ask for permission to obtain access at the Town Hall if the castle is closed. Just below the castle is the peaceful church of Nuestra Señora de la Asunción.

Aroche's main square, Plaza de España, has a good number of café-bars and is a delightful place to while away a few hours.

➕ 3B ✉ 33km (20 miles) west of Aracena 🍴 Bars and cafés in main square (€) 🚌 Regular service Aracena–Aroche ❓ *Semana Santa* (Holy Week), Mar/Apr; Pilgrimage of San Mamés, Whitsun; *Feria de Agosto*, Aug; Pilgrimage, Jun

CARMONA

Carmona stands on a high escarpment overlooking the fertile valleys of the Río Corbones and the Río Guadalquivir. Over 4km (2.5 miles) of ancient walls enclose old Carmona, and the main entrances to the town are through magnificent Roman gateways, the Puerta de Sevilla and the Puerta de Córdoba. The lively and sun-drenched Plaza de San Fernando, circular and fringed by trees, has some eye-catching buildings, and nearby is the market.

Follow narrow Calle Martín López de Córdoba out of Plaza de San Fernando to reach Santa María la Mayor church. The church is entered through the delightful Patio de los Naranjos, the entrance patio of the mosque that originally stood here, still with its orange trees and horseshoe arches. The church has a soaring Gothic nave and powerful *retablo*. Uphill, Calle G Freire leads to the superbly located Alcázar del Rey de Pedro, now an exclusive *parador*.

The Seville Gate incorporates the Moorish Alcázar de Abajo, where Carmona's tourism office is located. Beyond the gate, across Plaza Blas Infante, is modern Carmona, with its handsome church of San Pedro, whose tower replicates the style of Seville's Giralda. A wide promenade leads to Carmona's Roman Necropolis, one of Andalucía's chief archaeological sites.

www.turismo.carmona.org

➕ 6D ✉ 38km (24 miles) east of Seville 🛈 St Arco de la Puerta de Sevilla ☎ 954 19 09 55

ÉCIJA

This Ciudad de las Torres (City of Towers) is all dramatic skyline. Eleven magnificent church towers, steepled, domed and exquisitely decorated with colourful tiles, punctuate the sky, each with its resident storks. The town is much more than its towers, of course. There are remarkable 18th-century façades, so fluid in their forms that they hint at the work of Barcelona's Antoni Gaudí. Track down the Palacio de Peñaflor in Calle Castellar. It is a remarkable building, painted and sinuous and with a flamboyant baroque portal, lacking only a wider street to set if off. The Palacio de Benameji in Calle Cánovas del Castillo, home to the tourist office and a town museum, is another delight. Écija's splendid central square – the Plaza Mayor, or Plaza de España – has been walled off for the construction of an underground car park, which has robbed the encircling arcades and pleasant cafés of light and air; all the more reason to admire the glorious church towers.

www.turismoecija.com

✛ 7D ✉ 80km (50 miles) east of Seville

🚌 Regular service Seville–Écija

❓ *Semana Santa* (Holy Week), Mar/Apr; *Feria de Primavera* (Spring Fair), 8 May

ℹ️ Sq de España 1 ☎ 955 90 29 33

HUELVA

Huelva is the fourth-largest port in Spain. The city has paid a price for centuries of industry and commerce, and displays a grim approach from any direction. Yet its heart has great charm and life. The palm-fringed main square, Plaza de las Monjas, is surrounded by busy streets. A short distance east along the arcaded Avenida Martín Alonso Pinzón, in Alameda Sundheim, is Huelva's impressive Museo Provincial. Northeast is the curious Barrio Reina Victoria, or the Barrio Inglés, an Anglicized complex of housing, a legacy of the Río Tinto company.

🚩 2D 🖂 90km (56 miles) west of Seville 🚉 Estación de Ferrocarril, Avenida de Italia ☎ 902 24 02 02 🚌 Estación de Autobuses, Avenida de Portugal 9 ☎ 959 25 69 00 ℹ Plaza Alcalde Coto de Mora 2 ☎ 959 65 02 00

MOGUER

Moguer is one of the smartest and friendliest towns in Andalucía. The pretty central square, Plaza Cabildo, has a superb neo-classical Town Hall, framed by palm trees. Opposite, in a little square, there is a bronze bust of Juan Ramón Jiménez, a native son and a Nobel Prize-winning poet. A museum dedicated to him is at his birthplace, Calle Jiménez 5. The 14th-century Convento Santa Claraln, in nearby Plaza de las Monjas, is a museum and art gallery with a Mudéjar-style cloister and delightful church, still used for worship. Adjoining it is the splendid Convento de San Francisco.

www.aytomoguer.es

🚩 3D 🖂 15km (9 miles) east of Huelva 🚌 Regular service Huelva–Moguer ℹ Castillo s/n ☎ 959 37 18 98

a drive through the Sierra Norte

This drive takes you through the lesser-known parts of Seville province: the remote Parque Natural de la Sierra Norte.

Leave Carmona by the Seville Gate and follow signs for Lora del Río on the A457. After 20km (12 miles), go left at a junction. Cross the Río Guadalquivir and the railway line, then go left on the A431 to a junction before Alcalá del Río. Take the first exit (signed C433 Burguillos and Castilblanco). Stay on the C433 to Castilblanco, then follow signs for Cazalla de la Sierra on the C433.

You are now entering the Parque Natural de la Sierra Norte. The road winds through lonely hills swathed in cork oak, holm oak, pine and chestnut. Vulture, eagle and black stork are found here, and deer, wild boar, wild cat and mountain goat haunt the woodlands and rocky tops.

At a junction with the A432 go left (signed El Pedroso). At El Pedroso go right at a roundabout (signed A432 Constantina, Cazalla de la Sierra). Cross the railway and follow signs to Cazalla.

Cazalla de la Sierra is a pleasant country town, famous for its cherry brandy.

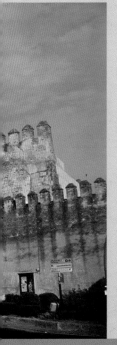

Leave Cazalla from its northern end, following signs for Constantina on the A455. Drive through wooded countryside, cross the railway at the isolated Constantina station and continue to Constantina.

Constantina is dominated by the medieval Castillo de la Armada, on a high hill, and has a charming old quarter.

Continue south from Constantina on the A455 to Lora del Río. Re-cross the railway line, then retrace your route back to Carmona.

Distance 220km (135 miles)
Time 8 hours, with stops
Start/end point Carmona ✚ 6D
Lunch Restaurante del Moro (€)
✉ c/ Paseo El Moro, Carmona
☎ 954 88 43 26

HOTELS

ARACENA
Finca Valbono (€€)
Situated in pleasant surroundings just outside Aracena, this old farmhouse has been tastefully converted into a small hotel with a restaurant, pool and riding stables.

✉ Carretera de Carboneras, Km 1 ☎ 959 12 77 11; www.fincavalbono.com

AROCHE
Hostal Picos de Aroche (€)
A friendly and immaculate establishment.

✉ Carretera Aracena 12 ☎ 959 14 04 75

CARMONA
Parador de Carmona (€€€)
Few hotels are as imposing as the 14th-century Arabic hilltop fortress that Carmona's *parador* occupies. Rooms have every modern feature but the *parador* retains the traditional interior courtyards and a spectacular dining room with an arched ceiling. Facilities include a swimming pool.

✉ c/ Alcázar s/n ☎ 954 14 10 10; www.parador.es

Pensión El Comercio (€)
Attractive, small pension built into the walls of the Puerta de Sevilla, the magnificent western gateway to the town.

✉ c/ Torre del Oro 56 ☎ 954 14 00 18

HUELVA
Luz Huelva (€€€)
A large, luxurious hotel near the museum and railway station.

✉ Alameda Sundheim 26 ☎ 959 25 00 11; www.nh-hoteles.com

MOGUER
Hostal Pedro Alonso Niño (€)
Outstanding value at this delightful little *hostal*, with its tiled patio and comfortable ensuite rooms with TV. Friendly owners.

✉ c/ Pedro Alonso Niño 13 ☎ 959 37 23 92

Hostal Platero (€)

Pleasant *hostal* named after the hero of Juan Ramón Jimenez's famous book, *Platero and I*, and close to the centre of the town.

✉ c/ Aceña 4 ☎ 959 37 21 59

OSUNA
El Caballo Blanco (€€)

This old coaching inn, a fascinating building, retains its arched entranceway and stableyard, where guests park their cars – a great advantage here. Pleasant rooms and good restaurant.

✉ c/ Granada 1 ☎ 954 81 01 84

SEVILLE
Las Casas del Rey de Baeza (€€€)

A city-centre boutique hotel, Las Casas manages to retain some sort of serenity with a rooftop pool, a cool whitewashed interior and minimal decoration. It's a good base for exploring the city.

✉ c/ Santiago ☎ 954 56 14 96; www.hospes.es

Hotel Alfonso XIII (€€€)

Very expensive, luxurious world-class hotel, built in 1928. The Moorish interiors are the last word in elegance and lavishness and there is an excellent restaurant open to non-residents.

✉ San Fernando 2 ☎ 954 91 70 00; www.alonsoxiii.com

Hotel Amadeus (€€)

Former 18th-century mansion, beautifully restored and decorated. With pianos in several soundproof rooms and concerts sometimes held in the foyer, this small hotel draws in musicians and music lovers. The terrace offers good views

✉ c/ Farnesio ☎ 954 50 14 43; www.hotelamadeussevilla.com

Hotel Simón (€€)

A well-placed city-centre hotel, just off the Avenida de la Constitución and near the cathedral. Once a private mansion, the hotel retains its period style, with a handsome patio and staircases.

✉ c/ García de Vinuesa 19 ☎ 954 22 66 60

RESTAURANTS

ARACENA

Casas (€€)

Well-run, prize-winning restaurant specializing in traditional Sierra Morena cuisine. Impressive wine list. The restaurant is on the way up to the Gruta de la Maravillas.

✉ Casas Colmenitas 41 ☎ 959 12 82 12 🕐 Lunch and dinner

AYAMONTE

Parador de Ayamonte (€€€)

Superb restaurant within this magnificent *parador*, with its sweeping views of the river. Try the regional seafood specialities such as *calamar relleno* (stuffed squid) and *raya en pimiento* (stingray with red pepper).

✉ El Castillito (Ayamonte) ☎ 959 32 07 00 🕐 Lunch and dinner

CARMONA

Alcázar del Rey Don Pedro (€€€)

This restaurant in Carmona's handsome *parador* is open to non-residents and serves high-quality local specialities and international dishes. Reservations are advised.

✉ Alcázar, s/n ☎ 954 14 10 10 🕐 Lunch and dinner

La Almazara de Carmona (€€)

Moorish décor in a pleasant restaurant on the eastern side of town. There is a good selection of salads and vegetable dishes using fresh local produce. The home-made desserts are particularly excellent.

✉ Santa Anna 33 ☎ 954 19 00 76 🕐 Lunch and dinner

ECIJA

Bodegón del Gallego (€€)

Located just round the corner from the Palacio de Peñaflor, this popular and well-run restaurant offers good fish dishes. Pick your own lobster, if you can bear to, from a display tank. Reservations are advised.

✉ c/ Arcipreste Aparicio 3 ☎ 954 83 26 18 🕐 Lunch and dinner

HUELVA
Taberna El Condado (€)
This lively tapas bar in the old part of town has a rustic flavour and is popular with locals.

✉ c/ Sor Ángela de la Cruz 3 ☎ 959 26 11 23 🕐 Lunch and dinner. Closed Sun

MOGUER
Mesón El Lobito (€)
El Lobito is housed in a cavernous building, where the walls are dense with the graffiti of patrons' names and initials. Alongside the bar is a huge open fire, on which food is expertly grilled.

✉ c/ Rábida 31 ☎ 959 37 06 60 🕐 Lunch and dinner

La Parrala (€)
See page 59.

OSUNA
Casa Curro (€)
This pleasant bar-restaurant in a small attractive square has an excellent tapas bar and a good menu. A favourite with locals.

✉ Plaza Salitre 5–9 ☎ 955 82 07 58 🕐 Breakfast, lunch and dinner

Doña Guadalupe (€)
Popular restaurant on a small square. It has a good reputation for its cuisine and a pleasant patio for outdoor eating.

✉ Plaza Guadalupe 6 ☎ 954 81 05 58 🕐 Lunch and dinner. Closed Mon and Tues

SEVILLE
Bar Giralda (€–€€)
See page 58.

Casa Robles (€€)
Family-run restaurant dating from the early 50s, a short walk from the cathedral. The *azulejo*-clad walls are typically Andalucían – as is the cuisine, including fish soup, hake and Serrano ham.

✉ c/ Álvarez Quintero 58 ☎ 954 21 31 50 🕐 Lunch and dinner

Corral del Agua (€–€€)

Housed in a former 18th-century mansion in the Santa Cruz district, this restaurant features a delightful plant-filled courtyard for dining out in the summer. The cuisine comprises tasty Andalucían-style dishes.

✉ Callejón del Agua 6 ☎ 954 22 48 41 🕓 Lunch and dinner. Closed Sun, Jan and 2 weeks in Feb

La Cueva (€€)

Patio restaurant at the heart of the Santa Cruz area. Excellent fish dishes, *paella* and lamb specialities.

✉ c/ Rodrigo Caro 18 ☎ 954 21 31 43 🕓 Lunch and dinner

Enrique Becerra (€€)

Attractive eatery with an international reputation, between Plaza Nueva and the bullring. Try the *salade de pâtes et crabe* (pasta and spider crab salad), or roasted lamb with honey and spinach and pine seed stuffing.

✉ c/ Gamazo 2 ☎ 954 21 30 49 🕓 Lunch and dinner. Closed Sun

El Giraldillo (€€)

Great tapas selection in this popular restaurant in sight of Seville's cathedral. Try the eggs 'flamenco style', a subtle mix of eggs, tomatoes, garlic onions and salami. Excellent *gazpacho*.

✉ Plaza Virgen de los Reyes 2 ☎ 954 21 45 25 🕓 Lunch and dinner

Hotel Alfonso XIII (€€€)

Dining here demands serious money, but the surroundings might just make you feel like a millionaire. Lunch is less of a drain on resources and offers an excellent choice.

✉ c/ San Fernando 2 ☎ 954 91 70 00 🕓 Lunch and dinner

Modesto (€)

Great fish and seafood restaurant in the southeast of Santa Cruz. Outside terrace where you can enjoy a good selection of tapas and *raciones* from the menu.

✉ c/ Cano y Cueto 5 🕓 Lunch and dinner

El Rincón de Pepe (€€)

El Rincón de Pepe is located in a handsome 19th-century house at the heart of Santa Cruz. There's fine *azulejos* tiling in the dining room and you can also eat out on the patio. It's noted for *paella* and fried fish dishes.

✉ c/ Gloria 6 🕐 Lunch and dinner

SHOPPING

ART AND CRAFTS

Artesanía Pascual

A wonderful craft shop with a great range of artefacts and potential gifts, and a friendly owner. You'll find it just behind the car park.

✉ Plaza de San Pedro 47, Aracena ☎ 959 12 80 07

Artesanía Textil

This fascinating shop sells an intriguing selection of gift items, such as wall hangings, hand-embroidered tablecloths and place mats.

✉ c/ Sierpes 70, Seville ☎ 954 56 28 40

Cerámica San Blas

A fine, working pottery tucked away down a quiet side street, complete with a modern pottery oven that radiates even more heat just inside the entrance door.

✉ c/ Dominguez de la Haza 18, Carmona ☎ 954 14 40 49

Ferretería Arte

An astonishing collection of rural and domestic ironmongery that is worth a browse even if you don't need anything.

✉ Carrera 17–19, Osuna ☎ 954 81 09 07

Modas Muñoz

This is the place to go for Sevillian dress. Buy up on *mantoncillos*, flamenco scarves, veils, shawls and the sort of shoes that get your heels tapping.

✉ Cerrajería 5, Seville ☎ 954 22 85 96

Sargadelos

Spanish homewares, specifically beautiful Galician ceramics and other items, are sold in this gallery-outlet. The boldly patterned ceramics are made at Sargadelos's own factory in Spain. The shop also organizes arts events and talks.

✉ Albareda 17, Seville ☎ 954 21 67 08; www.sargadelos.com

BOOKSHOPS
Vértice

International bookshop in the university area of Seville. Maps, guides and general books in many languages.

✉ c/ San Fernando 33, Seville ☎ 954 21 16 54

FASHION
Agua de Sevilla

Very stylish perfumery and accessories shop tucked away in Santa Cruz and near the Alcázar.

✉ Rodrigo Caro 16, Seville ☎ 954 22 43 56

Juan Foronda

Recreate your favourite flamenco performances with clothes from this historic city-centre shop. Delicate lace shawls, bright dresses and every imaginable flamenco accessory have been sold by Juan Foronda since 1926.

✉ c/ Tetuán 28 ☎ 954 22 60 60; www.juanforonda.com

FOOD AND DRINK
Jamones y Embeutidos Ibéricos, La Trastiendsa

The real *jamón negra* or *pata negra* of the Sierra Morena is on sale here, as well as a range of other speciality Spanish meat products.

✉ Plaza San Pedro 2, Aracena ☎ 959 12 71 58

JEWELLERY
Casa Ruiz

High-quality jewellery and silverware in two shops.

✉ O'Donnell 14, Seville ☎ 954 22 21 37 ✉ Sierpes 68, Seville
☎ 954 22 77 80

ENTERTAINMENT

NIGHTLIFE
Fun Club
With all types of music, ranging from Latin American to jazz. Live bands at the weekend. A great place for dance enthusiasts.

✉ Alameda de Hércules 86, Seville ☎ 650 48 98 58; www.salafunclub.com

FLAMENCO
El Arenal
A lavish flamenco theatre and restaurant with stage shows, with or without meal. This is very much set-piece flamenco, but it's well done and enjoyable. It caters mainly for coach parties, but individual reservations can be made. Book ahead.

✉ c/ Rodo 7, Seville ☎ 954 21 64 92; www.tablaoelarenal.com 🕓 Daily 9pm, 11:30pm

Los Gallos
Although this is a smaller venue than El Arenal, it still has a good and lively atmosphere.

✉ Plaza de Santa Cruz, Seville ☎ 954 21 69 81; www.tablaolosgallos.com 🕓 Daily 9pm, 11:30pm

SPORTS AND ACTIVITIES

HORSE-BACK RIDING
Doñana Ecuestre
Day-long rides through marshland.

✉ El Rocío, Parque Natural de Doñana ☎ 959 44 24 74; www.donanaecuestre.com

BIRD-WATCHING
The Coto de Doñana National Park has a wealth of resident wildlife and migratory birds, the latter especially in spring and autumn. Four-wheel drive tours are available at the visitor centre. Bird-watching trips are organised by Discovering Donaña, tel 959 44 24 66 or 620 96 43 69; www.discoveringdonana.com.

✉ Doñana Visitor Centre, Parque Nacional Coto de Doñana ☎ 959 44 23 40; jeep tour reservations 959 43 04 32

Index

air travel 26–27
Advance Passenger
    Information (API) 23
    domestic 28
Albaicín 102–103, 108–109
La Alcazaba, Almería 112–113
La Alcazaba, Málaga 134
Alcázar de los Reyes Cristianos
    80
Alhama de Granada 110
La Alhambra 36–37
Almería 60, 110–113
Almería province see Granada
    and Almería provinces
Almuñécar 71, 114
Las Alpujarras 38–39, 116–117
amusement parks 63
animal parks 62, 63
Antequera 138
Aqualand 62
Arab Baths, Granada 104
Arab Baths, Jaén 85
Arab Baths, Jerez de la
    Frontera 43
Arab Baths, Ronda 148
Arab Baths, Segura de la Sierra
    89
Aracena 40–41, 172
Archaeological Museum,
    Córdoba 81
Archaeological Museum,
    Granada 107
Archaeological Museum, Jerez
    de la Frontera 43
Archaeological Museum, Seville
    171
Arcos de la Frontera 138
Aroche 172–173

Baelo Claudio 149
Baeza 82–83
Balcón de Europa 71, 147
banks 32
Baños de la Encina 83
Barrio Santa Cruz 64–65, 167
Bayárcal 39
beaches and resorts 70–71
Benalmádena Costa 144
Bérchules 39
bird-watching 66, 71, 185
bodegas 42
Bubión 39, 116
bullfighting 89, 148
Bullfighting Museum, Córdoba
    81

Bullfighting Museum, Ronda
    148
buses 28

Cabo de Gata 71
Cádiz 60, 71, 72, 139–143
    Catedral Nueva 140
    Museo de Cádiz 140–141
    Museo Iconográfico e
        Histórico 141
    old town 142
    Oratorio de San Felipe Neri
        141
Cádiz province see Málaga and
    Cádiz provinces
camping 100
canoeing 100, 164
Capileira 39
Capilla Real 104–105
car rental 29
Carmona 60, 173
La Casa de Pilatos 168
Casa Natal de Picasso 135
casas colgadas 119
Castillo de Gibralfaro 135
cathedral, Almería 113
cathedral, Cádiz 140
cathedral, Granada 105
cathedral, Málaga 136
cathedral, Seville 168–169
Cave of the Bats 89
cave dwellings 115
Cave Museum 115
caving 164
Cazalla de la Sierra 177
Cazorla 60, 68, 84
ceramics 72, 119
children's entertainment 62–63
climate and seasons 22
concessions 28–29
Constantina 177
Córdoba 44–45, 60, 78–81
    Alcázar de los Reyes
        Cristianos 80
    Juderia 81
    Medina Azahara 78
    La Mezquita 44–45, 69
    Museo Arqueológico
        Provincial 81
    Museum of Bullfighting 81
Córdoba and Jaén provinces
    77–100
    entertainment 99–100
    hotels 92–93
    restaurants 94–97

shopping 98–99
sights 78–91
sports and activities 100
Costa de la Luz 71
Costa del Sol 70–71, 144
Costa Tropical 71, 114
crime 32
Crocodile Park 62
Cueva de los Murciélagos 89
Cueva Museo 115
Cuevas de Nerja 147
Cuevas de Sorbas 119
currency 30

drinking water 32
drives
    Las Alpujarras 116–117
    Parque Natural Sierra de
        Grazalema 150–151
    Sierra Norte 176–177
    Sierras 86–87
driving 22, 27, 29
drugs and medicines 32

Écija 174
economy 11
electricity 32
Embalse de Zahara 54
embassies and consulates 31
Las Empanadas 88
entertainment
    Córdoba and Jaén provinces
        99–100
    Granada and Almería
        provinces 129–130
    Málaga and Cádiz provinces
        161–162
    Seville and Huelva provinces
        185
Estepona 70–71, 144

Ferdinand and Isabella 50, 54,
    102, 104–105
ferry services 27
festivals and events 24–25
Fine Arts Museum, Jaén 85
Fine Arts Museum, Seville
    170–171
flamenco 19, 43, 69, 100, 103,
    162, 185
Flamenco Museum 170
food and drink 12–15
    Andalucian cuisine 12–13,
        15, 19
    drinking water 32

gazpacho 15, 19
jamón serrano 19, 39, 72
sherry 14, 42, 72
shopping for 99, 129, 160
wines and spirits 14
see also restaurants
football 66
Fuengirola 60, 144

gazpacho 15, 19
geography 10–11
Gibraltar 144
golf 67, 130, 163
Granada 102–109
  Albaicín 102–103, 108–109
  La Alhambra 36–37
  Baños Árabes 104
  Capilla Real 104–105
  catedral 105
  Monasterio de la Cartuja 107
  Monasterio de San Jerónimo 106–107
  Museo Arqueológico 107
Granada and Almería provinces 101–130
  entertainment 129–130
  hotels 120–123
  restaurants 123–127
  shopping 127–129
  sights 102–119
  sports and activities 130
Grazalema 145
Great Mosque of Córdoba 44–45
Grotto of Marvels 40–41
Gruta de las Maravillas 40–41
Guadalquivir 90–91
Guadix 114–115

hang-gliding 164
'hanging houses' 119
health 22, 23, 31–32
hiking and trekking 100, 164
horse-riding 66, 100, 162–163, 185
hot springs 110
hot-air ballooning 164
hotels
  Córdoba and Jaén provinces 92–93
  Granada and Almería provinces 120–123
  Málaga and Cádiz provinces 152–155

Seville and Huelva provinces 178–179
Huelva 175
Huelva province *see* Seville and Huelva provinces

Iconographic and Historical Museum 141
industry 11
insurance 22, 23
internet access 31
Itálica 170

Jaén 84–85
Jaén province *see* Córdoba and Jaén provinces
jamón serrano 19, 39, 72
Jerez de la Frontera 42–43
Judería 81

kitesurfing 71

language 33

Málaga 60, 132–137
  La Alcazaba 134
  Casa Natal de Picasso 135
  Castillo de Gibralfaro 135
  catedral 136
  Museo de Artes y Tradiciones Populares 136–137
  Museo Picasso 137
  sports and activities 162–164
Málaga and Cádiz provinces 131–164
  entertainment 161–162
  hotels 152–155
  restaurants 155–159
  shopping 159–161
  sights 132–151
Marbella 71, 144
markets 60
medical treatment 23
Medina Azahara 78
Medina Sidonia 146
Menga and Viera Dolmens 138
La Mezquita 44–45, 69
Mirador de San Nicolás 68, 103, 109
Mirador de las Ventanillas 46
Moguer 175
Mojácar 71, 115
Monasterio de la Cartuja 107
Monasterio de San Jerónimo 106–107

money 30
Montefrío 118
mountain biking 67, 100, 164
Mulhacén 11, 69, 116
Murillo Museum 64
museum and monument opening hours 32
museums
  Cueva Museo 115
  Museo de Alfarería 52
  Museo Arqueológico, Granada 107
  Museo Arqueológico, Jerez de la Frontera 43
  Museo Arqueológico, Seville 171
  Museo Arqueológico Provincial 81
  Museo de Artes y Tradiciones Populares 136–137
  Museo del Baile Flamenco 170
  Museo de Bellas Artes, Jaén 85
  Museo de Bellas Artes, Seville 170–171
  Museo de Cádiz 140–141
  Museo de Costumbres Populares 171
  Museo Iconográfico e Histórico 141
  Museo de Murillo 64
  Museo Picasso 137
  Museo Provincial 85
  Museum of Bullfighting, Córdoba 81
  Museum of Bullfighting, Ronda 148

national holidays 24
nature reserves 71
Neolithic burial sites 118, 138
Nerja 71, 147
Níjar 118–119

Oasys 62
opening hours 32
Oratorio de San Felipe Neri 141
Órgiva 60

Palace of the Christian Kings 80
Palacio de Peñaflor 174
Pampaneira 39
paragliding 164
Parque Acuático Mijas 62

Parque de las Ciencias 62
Parque Nacional de Doñana 71, 185
Parque Natural de los Alcornocales 146
Parque Natural de Cazorla, Segura y Las Villas 84
Parque Natural de Karst en Yesos 119
Parque Natural Sierra de Grazalema 145, 150–151
Parque Natural de la Sierra Norte 177
Parque Natural el Torcal 46–47
passports and visas 22
Las Peñas de los Gitanos 118
personal safety 32
pharmacies 32
Picasso Museum 137
Picasso's Birthplace 135
Pilate's House 168
police 32
Popular Arts Museum 171
population 11
Poqueira Gorge 39
postal services 31
Pottery Museum 52
Priego de Córdoba 48–49, 68
public transport 28–29
pueblos blancos 17, 54
Puerto Banús 144

Real Escuela Andaluza del Arte Ecuestre 43, 163
Reales Alcázares 50–51
Reserva Zoologica 62
restaurants 58–59
 Córdoba and Jaén provinces 94–97
 Granada and Almería provinces 123–127
 Málaga and Cádiz provinces 156–159
 Seville and Huelva provinces 180–183
rock-climbing 100, 164
Roman Necropolis 173
Ronda 148
Royal Andalucían School of Equestrian Art 43, 163
Royal Chapel, Granada 104–105
Royal Palaces, Seville 50–51

Salobreña 71, 114
San Pedro de Alcántara 144

Sanlúcar de Barrameda 60
Science Park 62
scuba-diving 67, 130, 164
Sea Life 63
Segura de la Sierra 88–89
Selwo Aventura 63
Seneca 81
Seville 50–51, 60, 64–65, 166–171
 Barrio Santa Cruz 64–65, 167
 La Casa de Pilatos 168
 La Catedral y La Giralda 168–169
 entertainment 185
 Itálica 170
 María Luisa Park 171
 Museo Arqueológico 171
 Museo del Baile Flamenco 170
 Museo de Bellas Artes 170–171
 Museo de Costumbres Populares 171
 Plaza de España 171
 Reales Alcázares 50–51
Seville and Huelva provinces 165–185
 entertainment 185
 hotels 178–179
 restaurants 180–183
 shopping 183–184
 sights 166–177
 sports and activities 185
sherry 14, 42, 72
shopping
 best buys 72
 Córdoba and Jaén provinces 98–99
 Granada and Almería provinces 127–129
 Málaga and Cádiz provinces 159–161
 markets 60
 opening hours 32
 Seville and Huelva provinces 183–184
Sierra de Cazorla 88, 100
Sierra de Contraviesa 38
Sierra de Gádor 39
Sierra de Grazalema 145, 150–151
Sierra de Las Villas 88
Sierra Norte 176–177
Sierra de Segura 88

Sierra Subbética 89
skiing 130
Sorbas 119
Sorbas Caves 119
Sotogrande 144
sports and activities 66–67, 100, 130, 162–164, 185
student and young travellers 28–29
sun safety 31
swimming 67
synagogue, Córdoba 81

Tarifa 68, 71, 149
taxis 28
telephones 31
tennis 67
theme park 62
time differences 23
tipping 30
TivoliWorld 63
Torre del Vinaigre 86, 88
Torremolinos 144
tourist information 23, 30
train services 27, 28
travel arrangements 26–27
Trevélez 39

Úbeda 52–53

Vejer de la Frontera 149
views 68–69

walks
 Albaicín, Granada 108–109
 Barrio Santa Cruz, Seville 64–65
 old Cádiz 142
 Río Guadalquivir 90–91
water parks 62
websites 23
whale- and dolphin-spotting 63
'white towns' 17, 54
windsurfing 67, 68, 71, 164
wines 14

La Yedra 68, 84
Yegen 39

Zahara de la Sierra 54–55
Zoo Fuengirola 63
Zuheros 89

Acknowledgements

The Automobile Association would like to thank the following photographers, companies and picture libraries for their assistance in the preparation of this book.

Abbreviations for the picture credits are as follows – (t) top; (b) bottom; (c) centre; (l) left; (r) right; (AA) AA World Travel Library.

4l Velez Blanco, AA/D Robertson; **4c** Alhambra, AA/J Edmanson; **4r** Reales Alcazares, AA/A Molyneux; **5l** Nerja, AA/M Chaplow; **5r** Plaza de Espana, AA/D Robertson; **6/7** Velez Blanco, AA/D Robertson; **8/9** Guitarist in Cordoba, AA/M Chaplow; **10t** Gilded statue of the Virgin in the church of San Felipe Neri in Cadiz, AA/D Robertson; **10b** Beach at Mojacar, AA/J Edmanson; **10/1** Castle at Salobrena, AA/J Tims; **11** Castle on Gibralfaro Hill, AA/J Edmanson; **12** Seafood vendor, AA/D Robertson; **13tl** Orange tree, AA/J Edmanson; **13tr** Seafood Dish, AA/A Molyneux; **13cl** Barbecued fish, AA/J Tims; **13b** Spices, AA/M Chaplow; **14** Wine barrels, AA/P Wilson; **14/5** Marketplace, AA/M Chaplow; **15t** Spices, AA/M Chaplow; **16** Giralda Tower in Seville, AA/M Chaplow; **16/7** Mosaic tiles in Alhambra in Granada, AA/J Edmanson; **17t** Zahara de la Sierra, AA/M Chaplow; **17b** Café, AA/M Chaplow; **18/9** Flamenco show, AA/M Jordan; **19** Wine barrels, AA/P Wilson; **20/1** Alhambra, AA/J Edmanson; **24/5** Children at a festival, AA/D Robertson; **27t** Seville Airport, AA/A Molyneux; **27b** coach driver at the Mezquita in Cordoba, AA/D Robertson; **28/9** Taxi rank, AA/A Molyneux; **31t** Postbox, AA/M Chaplow; **31b** Telephone box, AA/M Chaplow; **32** Policeman, AA/J Tims; **34/5** Ambassador's Hall in in the Reales Alcazares, AA/A Molyneux; **36** La Alhambra, AA/D Robertson; **36/7** La Alhambra, AA/D Robertson; **38/9t** Las Alpujarras, AA/D Robertson; **38/9** Bubion in Las Alpujarras, AA/D Robertson; **40/1** Gruta de las Maravillas, MELBA PHOTO AGENCY/Alamy; **42** Royal Andalusian School of Equestrian Art in Jerez de la Frontera, AA/P Wilson; **42/3** Jerez de la Frontera, AA/J Edmanson; **43** Jerez de la Frontera, AA/M Chaplow; **44/5** La Mezquita, AA/D Robertson; **45** La Mezquita, AA/M Chaplow; **46** Parque Natural el Torcal, AA/M Chaplow; **47** Sierra del Torcal in the Parque Natural el Torcal, AA/M Chaplow; **48** Detail of the Fuente del Rey, AA/M Chaplow; **48/9** Fuente del Rey, AA/M Chaplow; **49** White washed house in Priego de Cordoba, AA/ M Chaplow; **50** Reales Alcazares in Seville, AA/A Molyneux; **50/1** Reales Alcazares in Seville, AA/A Molyneux; **52** Sacra Capilla del Salvador in Ubeda, AA/M Chaplow; **52/3t** House in Ubeda, AA/M Chaplow; **52/3b** Church of Santa Maria de los Reales Alcazares in Ubeda, AA/M Chaplow; **54/5** Zahara de la Sierra, AA/M Chaplow; **56/7** Nerja, AA/M Chaplow; **58** Restaurant, AA/D Robertson; **60/1** Vegetables for sale, AA/M Chaplow; **62** Almeria - Mini Hollywood, A/D Robertson; **64/5** Barrio Santa Cruz, AA/P Wilson; **66/7** Horse riding, AA/J Poulsen; **68/9** Antequara, AA/J Tims; **70** Beach, AA/J Tims; **73** Plates for sale, AA/M Chaplow; **74/5** Plaza de Espana, AA/D Robertson; **77** Baeza, AA/M Chaplow; **78** Waterfall at the Alcazar de los Reyes Cristianos in Cordoba, AA/M Chaplow; **79** Alcazar, Cordoba, AA/M Chaplow; **80/1** Alcazar, Cordoba, AA/M Chaplow; **82** Baeza, AA/M Chaplow; **82/3** Baeza, AA/M Chaplow; **83** Banos de la Encina, AA/M Chaplow; **84** View of Cazorla, AA/M Chaplow; **84/5** Jaen, AA/M Chaplow; **86/7** Segura de la Sierra, AA/M Chaplow; **88/9** Segura de la Sierra, AA/M Chaplow; **90/1** Waterfall at Rio Guadalquivir, blickwinkel/Alamy; **101** Velez Blanco, AA/J Edmanson; **102/3** The Albaicin, AA/M Chaplow; **104/5** Capilla Real, AA/ D Robertson; **105** Capilla Real, AA/M Chaplow; **106/7** Convento de San Jeronimo, AA/M Chaplow; **108** Plaza Nueva, AA/M Chaplow; **110/11** Almeria, AA/D Robertson; **112/3** La Alcazaba de Almeira, AA/J Edmanson; **114/5** Salobrena AA/J Tims; **115** Guadix, AA/M Chaplow; **116/7** Las Alpujarras, AA/D Robertson; **118/9** Montefrio, AA/M Chaplow; **119** Nijar, AA/M Chaplow; **131** Ronda, AA/P Wilson; **132/3** View from Castle Gibralfaro, AA/J Tims; **134/5** La Alcazaba in Malaga, AA/P Wilson; **135** View of La Alcazaba and Castillo de Gibralfaro, AA/P Wilson; **136t** Cathedral in Malaga, AA/M Chaplow; **136b** Museo de Artes Y Tradiciones Populares, AA/J Poulsen; **136/7** Museo de Artes Y Tradiciones Populares, AA/J Poulsen; **138** Dolmen Cave in Antequara, AA/M Chaplow; **138/9** Cadiz, AA/P Wilson; **140** Cathedral in Cadiz, AA/P Wilson; **141** Oratorio de San Felipe Neri, AA/D Robertson; **143** Cadiz, AA/J Edmanson; **144/5** View over Gibraltar, AA/P Wilson; **146** Santa Maria la Coronada in Medina Sidonia, AA/M Chaplow; **146/7** Nerja, AA/J Tims; **148/9** Ronda, AA/D Robertson; **149** Tarifa, AA/P Wilson; **150/1** Parque Natural Sierra de Grazalema, AA/M Chaplow; **151t** Cork oak tree, AA/M Chaplow; **151b** Locally made crafts in Grazalema, AA/D Robertson; **165** Plaza de Espana in Seville, AA/D Robertson; **166/7** Plaza de Espana in Seville, AA/P Wilson; **167** Barrio Santa Cruz, AA/M Chaplow; **168** La Casa de Pilatos, AA/P Wilson; **168/9** Seville Cathedral, AA/P Wilson; **170/1t** Plaza de Espana in Seville, AA/J Edmanson; **170/1b** Maria Luisa Park, AA/J Edmanson; **171** Tile in the Plaza de Espana, AA/D Robertson; **172** Aracena, AA/D Robertson; **172/3b** Aracena, AA/D Robertson; **173** Carmona, AA/D Robertson; **174/5** Ecija, AA/D Robertson; **175** Huelva, AA/D Robertson; **176/7** Seville gate, Carmona, AA/M Chaplow.

Every effort has been made to trace the copyright holders, and we apologise in advance for any accidental errors. We would be happy to apply the corrections in the following edition of this publication.

Sight locator index

This index relates to the maps on the covers. We have given map references to the main sights of interest in the book. Grid references in italics indicate sights featured on town maps. Some sights within towns may not be plotted on the maps.

Albaicín, Granada *Granada 3b*

Alhama de Granada **19K**

Almería **22L**

Antequera **17K**

Aracena **4B**

Arcos de la Frontera **14J**

Aroche **3B**

Baeza **11D**

Baños Arabes *Granada 3b*

Baños de la Encina **11D**

Barrio Santa Cruz *Sevilla 3b*

Cádiz **13K**

Capilla Real *Granada 2c*

Carmona **6D**

Casa Natal de Picasso *Málaga 5a*

Castillo de Gibralfaro *Málaga 6c*

Catedral, Granada *Granada 2c*

Catedral, Málaga *Málaga 3c*

Cazorla **12E**

Córdoba **8D**

Costa del Sol **18L**

Costa Tropical **19L**

Écija **7D**

Gaudix **21K**

Gibraltar **15M**

Granada **20K**

Grazalema **15K**

Huelva **2D**

Itálica **5D**

Jaén **10E**

Jerez de la Frontera **13J**

La Alcazaba *Málaga 4c*

La Alhambra *Granada 4b*

La Casa de Pilatos *Sevilla 3a*

La Catedral y la Giralda *Sevilla 2b*

La Mezquita, Córdoba **8D**

Las Alpujarras **21K**

Málaga **18K**

Medina Sidonia **14K**

Moguer **3D**

Mojácar **24L**

Monasterio de la Cartuja *Granada 1a (off map)*

Monasterio San Jerónimo *Granada 1b (off map)*

Montefrío **19J**

Museo Arqueológico *Granada 3b*

Museo de Artes y Tradiciones Populares *Málaga 2a*

Museo de Bellas Artes *Sevilla 2a*

Museo del Baile Flamenco *Sevilla 2a*

Museo Picasso *Málaga 4b*

Nerja **19L**

Níjar **23L**

Plaza de España & María Luisa Park *Sevilla 3c*

Priego de Córdoba **19J**

Reales Alcázares *Sevilla 2b*

Ronda **16K**

Segura de la Sierra **23G**

Seville **5D**

Sierras de Cazorla, Segura y las Villas **23H**

Sorbas **24L**

Tarifa **14M**

Úbeda **12D**

Vejer de la Frontera **13L**

Zahara de la Sierra **15K**

Zuheros **19H**

Dear Reader

Your comments, opinions and recommendations are very important to us. So please help us to improve our travel guides by taking a few minutes to complete this simple questionnaire.

You do not need a stamp (unless posted outside the UK). If you do not want to cut this page from your guide, then photocopy it or write your answers on a plain sheet of paper.

Send to: **The Editor, AA World Travel Guides,
FREEPOST SCE 4598, Basingstoke RG21 4GY.**

Your recommendations...

We always encourage readers' recommendations for restaurants, nightlife or shopping – if your recommendation is used in the next edition of the guide, we will send you a **FREE AA Guide** of your choice from this series. Please state below the establishment name, location and your reasons for recommending it.

_____

_____

_____

_____

_____

_____

Please send me **AA Guide** _____

About this guide...

Which title did you buy?

AA _____

Where did you buy it? _____

When? m m / y y

Why did you choose this guide? _____

_____

_____

_____

_____

Did this guide meet your expectations?

Exceeded ☐   Met all ☐   Met most ☐   Fell below ☐

Were there any aspects of this guide that you particularly liked? _____

_____

_____

_____

continued on next page...

Is there anything we could have done better? _____

_____

_____

_____

About you...

Name (*Mr/Mrs/Ms*) _____

Address _____

_____

_____ Postcode _____

Daytime tel nos _____

Email _____

Please only give us your mobile phone number or email if you wish to hear from us about other products and services from the AA and partners by text or mms, or email.

Which age group are you in?
Under 25 ☐   25–34 ☐   35–44 ☐   45–54 ☐   55–64 ☐   65+ ☐

How many trips do you make a year?
Less than one ☐   One ☐   Two ☐   Three or more ☐

Are you an AA member? Yes ☐   No ☐

About your trip...

When did you book? m m / y y   When did you travel? m m / y y

How long did you stay? _____

Was it for business or leisure? _____

Did you buy any other travel guides for your trip? _____

If yes, which ones? _____

_____

_____

Thank you for taking the time to complete this questionnaire. Please send it to us as soon as possible, and remember, you do not need a stamp (*unless posted outside the UK*).

| **AA** Travel Insurance call 0800 072 4168 or visit www.theAA.com |

The information we hold about you will be used to provide the products and services requested and for identification, account administration, analysis, and fraud/loss prevention purposes. More details about how that information is used is in our privacy statement, which you'll find under the heading "Personal Information" in our terms and conditions and on our website: www.theAA.com. Copies are also available from us by post, by contacting the Data Protection Manager at AA, Fanum House, Basing View, Basingstoke, Hampshire RG21 4EA.

We may want to contact you about other products and services provided by us, or our partners (by mail, telephone or email) but please tick the box if you DO NOT wish to hear about such products and services from us by mail, telephone or email. ☐